Friendship
and
Finances
in Philippi

Friendship and Finances in Philippi

THE LETTER OF PAUL TO THE PHILIPPIANS

Ben Witherington III

THE NEW TESTAMENT IN CONTEXT

Howard Clark Kee and J. Andrew Overman, editors

TRINITY PRESS INTERNATIONAL
Valley Forge, Pennsylvania

Trinity Press International, P.O. Box 1321, Harrisburg, PA 17105

Library of Congress Cataloging-in-Publication Data

Witherington, Ben, 1951–
    Friendship and finances in Philippi : the letter of Paul to the
Philippians / Ben Witherington III.
       p. cm. — (New Testament in context)
    Includes bibliographical references and index.
    ISBN 1-56338-102-8 :
    1. Bible. N.T. Philippians—Commentaries. I. Title.
II. Series.
BS2705.3.W57 1994
227'.607—dc20   94-38399
                                                CIP

Printed in the United States of America

05 06 07 08 09   10 9 8 7 6 5 4 3 2

This book is dedicated to those congregations who have a sense of what unity and concord in the faith is really all about, and to those who understand that the communion of the saints involves a great deal more than a particular denominational expression of the church or a particular local church. Indeed, this communion extends backward in time two millennia, and outward geographically in all directions.

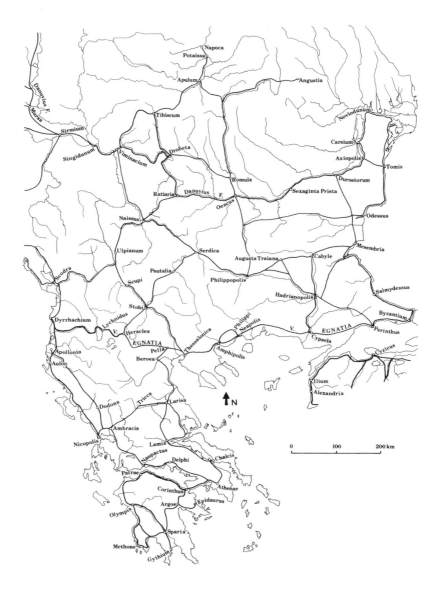

Major Roman roads of Greece, Macedonia, and the lower Danube
Used with permission from *Roman Bridges,* Colin O'Connor,
Cambridge University Press, 1993, p. 26

Philippi

Photo by Raymond Schoder, Courtesy of Biblical Archaeology Society

Via Egnatia

Photo by Raymond Schoder, Courtesy of Biblical Archaeology Society

A peasant may believe as much
As a great clerk, and reach the highest stature,
Thus dost thou make proud knowledge bend and crouch,
While grace fills up uneven nature.

— George Herbert
"Faith," stanza eight

Contents

Chapter One

Background and Foreground of Paul and the Philippian Letter

I. Paul

Paul was the product of the cross-fertilization of three cultural orientations — Jewish, Hellenistic Greek, and Roman.[1] The evidence suggests that he was a Roman citizen, as were his parents before him; that he was born in one of the centers of Hellenistic culture in the ancient world, Tarsus in Asia Minor; and that he was a child of orthodox Jews who took or sent him to Jerusalem at an early age to study at the feet of the notable teacher Gamaliel in order to become a good Pharisaic teacher.[2]

The Jewish influence is the most important for our discussion of Paul and his form of discourse, for W. C. Van Unnik has argued forcefully that the evidence from Acts suggests that Paul was taken to Jerusalem at a very early age and raised there.[3] Would this rule out Paul's having received basic training in Greco-Roman rhetoric? The answer is no, for even prominent teachers like Hillel before Paul's day were affected by the process of Hellenization that swept the entire region centuries before, as is shown by the rhetorical patterns of Jewish argumentation of this era.[4] E. A. Judge points out that half of Gamaliel's pupils are said to have been trained in the *sophia* of the Greeks, which would surely include rhetoric. Paul could certainly have been one of those who had received such training.[5] In addition, Pharisaism was a proselytizing religion (see Matt. 23:15)[6] and as such needed forms of argumentation and persuasion in the *lingua franca* of the day, Koine Greek. With such arguments they could

1

convince Diaspora Jews, and also some Gentiles, especially those who were already synagogue adherents.

Even if Paul did not grow up in Jerusalem but in Tarsus, the latter was not a cultural backwater, but rather a university town. In fact many felt that the university there surpassed those in Athens or Alexandria in the study of philosophy and literature.[7] Whether he received his primary education in Tarsus, or more likely in Jerusalem, Paul was in the upper 1–2 percent of well-educated people in his day. Only a notable minority of families would have been able to provide the opportunities for education that Paul's letters show that he had. It is thus important not to underestimate any of the apostle's life influences. Paul owed a considerable intellectual and personal debt to Greco-Roman culture and to Judaism, though it is fair to say that early Judaism had the strongest influence on him prior to his conversion to Christianity.[8]

Apparently, Jews in particular and provincials in general were not granted Roman citizenship very regularly, so we may surmise that Paul's family must have provided some service to the Empire to be granted this status. Perhaps they had made tents for the Roman army. Paul's Roman citizenship would have ensured him free access to the whole Mediterranean and beyond, and his citizenship likely protected him on occasion from local injustices and prejudices (see Acts 16:37). His citizenship may also account for his somewhat positive view of the Roman Empire and its system of justice (see Rom. 13; 2 Thess. 2:7). In any event, Paul took advantage of Roman roads, Roman justice, and Roman order once he became a missionary for Christ.

The diversity of Paul's background was good preparation for him to be an *apostolos* to Gentiles. It likely provided him with a broader view of Jews and Greeks, women and men, and slaves and free persons (see 1 Cor. 9:19ff.) than would have been the case if he had been raised in more narrowly Jewish circles in a small Galilean or Judean village in Israel, as some of the early Jewish Christians were. Paul knew something of how to be the Jew to the Jew and the Greek to the Greek, and this served him well once he found his Christian calling in life.

Paul's missionary strategy, at least by the late 40s, was to evangelize the major urban cities (e.g., Ephesus, the Roman colony of Philippi, Thessalonica, Corinth), most of which lay on major Roman roads. The image of Paul racing breathlessly around the Roman Empire, never staying in one place more than a few days or weeks, is to a significant degree a false one. Paul saw himself as a pioneer missionary whose chief task was to start Christian communities in places where they did not previously exist. He tended and intended to stay in a location long enough to accomplish that task well.[9]

Paul's familiarity with the larger world of Greco-Roman culture is evident from his use of Greek ideas *and* from the occasional allusions he makes to the Greek poets and philosophers (e.g., 1 Cor. 15:33), though it is difficult to know, since the quotations are few and far between, how profound Paul's knowledge was of Greek or Roman philosophical writings. A. J. Malherbe and others have shown that Paul reflects some acquaintance with Cynic, Stoic, and Epicurean thought, though they are not the *main* sources of his own teaching.[10] Nevertheless, at points the influence seems to be significant, for instance, in 2 Corinthians 10:3–6, and possibly in Philippians where Paul discusses the secret of contentment (4:10–13). On the whole I agree with the careful conclusion of Malherbe:

> It may well be the case that, when Paul is viewed as a theologian, the hellenistic elements do not lie at the center of his thinking, *but provide the means by which he conducts his argument.* But when he and others discuss his ministry, it is extraordinary to what degree the categories and language are derived from the Greeks.[11]

More clearly, Paul was influenced by Greek rhetorical style in the way he formed and developed his whole letters, not just in the use of occasional conventional rhetorical devices. Thus, one must assume some considerable Greek education. Rhetoric, unlike philosophy, was at the very heart of education, even secondary education, during the Empire, and Paul is likely to have been more indebted to it through his education than to Greek or Roman philosophy.[12] There is considerable evidence that even at the secondary level of education, where the focus was on systematic training in language and literature, some rhetoric was being taught by the *grammaticus*. One must not think of a rigid three-tiered system where rhetoric was reserved for only the third level of education: The great Roman rhetorician Quintilian complains about "grammarians" teaching the first parts of rhetoric before the student gets to the school of rhetoric.[13]

For Paul, these larger cultural influences were filtered through a Jewish and scriptural orientation — focusing on issues such as the law, messiah, and eschatology — and after Paul's experience on Damascus road, through a Jewish-*Christian* orientation. K. W. Niebuhr rightly stresses that Paul was most shaped in his early and middle years by his Jewish origins and faith.[14] Under some provocation Paul says in 2 Corinthians 11:21-22: "What anyone else dares to boast about, I am speaking as a fool, I also dare to boast about. Are they Hebrews? So am I. Are they Israelites? So am I. Are they Abraham's descendants? So am I" (see Phil. 3:4-6). Paul believed he had few peers in his pedigree.

As a Pharisee Paul had apparently trained under Gamaliel, one of the more broad-minded of early Jewish teachers, but Paul showed no such temperate character in his zeal against the fledgling Christian community. Rather, he was a zealot for God's law and its enforcement, and anyone who disputed that Jews should follow such a course he would adamantly oppose (see Gal. 1:13). The Pharisees in general were attempting to extend to all of God's people the Levitical standards of holiness, which in the OT were applied only to the priesthood. They wished to organize all of life, every human activity, in accord with God's Word. This included a concern about purity of diet, clothing, and religious observances such as prayer, fasting, and tithing. The Pharisees, unlike the Sadducees, accepted such ideas as resurrection of the righteous, eternal life and eternal death, and believed in angels and spirits (see Acts 23:8). Some believed that everything happens through the providence of God, though human beings also have moral responsibility. Most of these beliefs continued on in Paul's Christian life.

Even after Paul became a Jewish Christian, he still saw many advantages to being a Jew (see Rom. 3:1, 11:1ff.).[15] Yet Paul, whose Jewish name was Saul, also had reason to look back with regret on some of the things he did while an ardent Pharisaic Jew, particularly his persecution of the *ekklēsia*.[16] This is at least in part why later he felt unworthy to be called an *apostolos* (see 1 Cor. 15:9). In Galatians 1:13 Paul admits that he persecuted the church violently. He even went to foreign cities to try to persecute Christians because he felt they were undermining the validity of Judaism and, in particular, the law (see Acts 26:11). He was likely in his early twenties or even younger when he began such campaigns against Christians, though it is hard to tell whether or not he interrupted his studies with Gamaliel to undertake such tasks.

The Paul we meet in Philippians had been a Christian for as many as twenty-five years and thus was not an immature convert. He had long since left his earlier life behind. Here we meet an *apostolos* who had been fully engaged in his missionary activities for perhaps two decades.[17] To understand better the apostle and his letters we need to reflect on both his social world and his use of rhetoric.

II. Paul, His Letters, and His Rhetoric

This commentary is called a socio-rhetorical commentary because it will attempt to bring to bear insights not just from the area of the social sciences, but also from the detailed study of Greco-Roman rhetoric. Rhetorical criticism may be said to be a subspecies of literary criticism but with a decidedly historical interest. It reveals a great deal about how various NT authors structured their writings. Rhetoric is by definition the art of persuasion, and there were particular literary devices and forms that were used in antiquity to persuade the hearer or reader about some matter.[18] Attention to the rhetorical dimension of Paul's letters has revealed how certain forms of argument or exhortation function, and thus how they ought to be interpreted. Rhetoric has attracted so much attention of late because

> rhetorical criticism holds some promise for bridging biblical scholars' older, historical concerns and their newer,

literary interests.... Rhetorical criticism is forthrightly interested in texts: defining their limits, exploring their construction and disposition, assessing their style, probing the
salient issues that drive them in certain directions.... the
study of rhetoric attempts to understand more fully the
overt and subtle relationships that exist between the form
and content of texts, between those who generate and
those who receive such texts. [It]...does not intend to
be an ahistorical method of reading texts. Its *raison d'être*
stems in large measure from the fact that rhetoric was a systematic, academic discipline taught and practiced throughout the Greco-Roman world.[19]

Rhetorical-critical study of Paul's letters primarily involves the
study of the form and function of the text itself in comparison
with other ancient examples of rhetoric, and only secondarily,
if at all, is it concerned with larger contextual and social issues. Nonetheless, in what follows we will examine both the
social context and the rhetorical form of Paul's Philippian letter,[20] as well as offer some of the linguistic and historical data
one usually finds in biblical commentaries.[21]

The translations and basic textual discussions of the commentary are meant for a general audience that includes both college
and seminary Bible students, pastors, and educated lay persons;
I have tried to distill the benefits of these new disciplines for
them. The more detailed discussion for more advanced students
and scholars has been confined mainly either to the notes or
to the various detailed comments that are set apart in smaller
type. These may be passed over by those wishing to use the
commentary for an entry-level discussion.

Paul wrote his letters as necessary substitutes for oral communication. The evidence strongly suggests that he intended his
letters to be read aloud in the congregational meeting. The clo-
sure of 1 Corinthians 16:20 refers to the practice of the holy
kiss, a practice that was part of early Christian worship.[22] This
suggests that once the letter was read, the service was at or near-
ing completion. Second, at the end of Galatians Paul expects the
audience in general ("you" plural) to be able to see his handwrit-

ing at the end of the letter (Gal. 6:11), another clear sign the letter would be read in the public gathering of the worshipers. Third, the greetings that pepper the end of various of Paul's letters imply a meeting of the group where some of those named could hear such a greeting. Thus, the evidence of Colossians 4:16, whether written by Paul or another, certainly reflects the practice in the Pauline churches.

This is important when we turn to the matter of the rhetorical form of Paul's letters to the Philippians. A good deal of what he wrote was with the intention that it have a certain effect on the listening ear. The tendency to treat these documents simply as *texts* overlooks an important dimension of their intended function. Paul used the literary conventions of his day in two ways. On the one hand, his letters conform to a significant degree to the general structure of other ancient letters. On the other hand, Paul also chose to draw on the conventions of ancient Greco-Roman rhetoric in shaping his communications with his converts. We must discuss each in turn.

A. Philippians as a Letter

Letters in antiquity, with rare exception (e.g., Cicero), were not meant for the general public, much less for publication. They were considered an inadequate, though necessary, substitute for a face-to-face oral communication, and scholars have rightly emphasized the oral character of Paul's letters. Furthermore, Paul's letters are *group* communications, and even a more personal letter like Philemon is not a real exception since it is to be read in a house-church meeting.[23] This means they include what Paul is willing for *all* the congregation to hear, or at least overhear if he is singling out a member or group in the congregation. Paul is using letters as a not entirely satisfactory surrogate for face-to-face conversation (see Rom. 15:14–33, 1 Cor. 4:14–21, 1 Thess. 2:17–3:13, Gal. 4:12–20).

Ancient letters were quite terse and to the point. In this regard most of Paul's letters are very different from the average private letter in the first century, for Paul's are much longer than normal. Ancient letters from the fourth century B.C.E. to the fourth century C.E. could contain the following elements: (1) the name of the writer; (2) the name of the addressee; (3) a greeting; (4) the body of the letter, which included a thanksgiving or wish prayer and then an introductory formula followed by the substance of the letter, sometimes with an eschatological conclusion or a travelogue; (5) ethical or practical advice; and (6) a conclusion with final greetings and benediction (the writing process is sometimes mentioned as well). Parts of 4 and 5 above are usually found in Paul's correspondence but are uncommon in other ancient letters. The only Pauline letter that does not contain a thanksgiving prayer of some sort is Galatians, and its absence is notable, for Paul can think of little to be thankful for in view of what is happening to his churches in Galatia.

It is clear that when Paul wrote he used scribes, called amanuenses, like other writers in antiquity (Rom. 16:22). This is also evident when Paul says at the end of various letters that he is now taking up the pen to write a line and perhaps to add a characteristic signature (see 1 Cor. 16:21, Gal. 6:11, 2 Thess. 3:17). This raises questions about how much freedom Paul granted a scribe in composing the letter. Did Paul dictate word for word to his scribe; or did he dictate the sense and leave the formulation to the secretary; or did he even instruct a secretary or friend like Silas or Timothy to write for him on occasion without dictating specific content? Were Paul's scribes professionals or amateurs? Quintilian, the greatest teacher of rhetoric in the first century C.E., preferred not to use an amanuensis because it limited his freedom to rethink and revise out loud.

> For, when we write, however great our speed, the fact that the hand cannot follow the rapidity of our thoughts gives us time to think whereas the presence of our amanuensis hurries us on, and at times we feel ashamed to hesitate or pause, or make some alteration, as though we were afraid to display such weakness before a witness.... Again if the amanuensis is a slow writer, or lacking in intelligence, he becomes a stumbling-block, our speed is checked, and the thread of our ideas is interrupted by the delay or even per-

haps by the loss of temper to which it gives rise. (*Inst. Or.* 10.3.19–20)

Several things should be kept in mind. First, various of Paul's letters read like dictated documents expressing both the mind and very words of Paul. In fact, perhaps the reason why we sometimes have sentence fragments is that Paul is dictating so fast that the scribe is unable to keep up. Second, even if Paul left the formulation of the letter to a scribe, perhaps giving him the main ideas, 2 Thessalonians 3:17, 18 indicates that Paul signed all his letters, likely reviewing the document first. If so, it is not important whether or not we have Paul's exact vocabulary or words represented in each letter so long as we have his thoughts and directives.[24] Third, the evidence as it presents itself suggests that Paul usually dictated his letters verbatim but that in extenuating circumstances, such as when he was in prison, Paul likely gave a scribe more freedom to compose for him, after which he read the letter, made changes, and put his signature on it (e.g., possibly but not probably Philippians). Paul's letters were too important as an expression of his apostolic authority to allow words/ideas that were not consistent with his own thinking or intent to remain in a document that he would ultimately endorse.

Paul's letter carriers seem to have been entrusted with additional oral communication. Possibly, Paul intended for the messenger to explain or expand upon some of the letter.[25] Paul may have chosen couriers such as a Timothy or a Titus because they had the capacity to perform a letter orally in Greek in a way that conformed to Paul's rhetorical strategy and intent.

Paul's letters must be seen as part of a total communication effort that included letters, oral instructions through messengers, and face-to-face communication, whether preaching, teaching, or some form of dialogue. The dialogical character of many letters is evident, for a goodly portion of them are given over to answering questions that are addressed to Paul. This is particularly true in the case of 1 and 2 Corinthians, but it seems to be much less the case in Philippians, perhaps because Paul is far removed in time and/or distance from his converts, or because they have not written him with inquiries, other than about his well-being, and perhaps that of Epaphroditus. Nevertheless, it is essentially correct to say that Paul's letters are usually "conversations in context"[26] that address specific matters of concern for a particular group of Christians,[27] though they include directives and principles that can be applied in many other situations.

There must be a cautious balance between "treating Paul's letters as purely occasional, contextual writings, directed only to specific situations, and as attempts to express a Christian understanding of life which has ramifications for theological expression beyond the particular historical situation."[28] To a great extent Paul is drawing on not only preexisting mental resources but also preexisting forms in writing these letters. They are not purely ad hoc in character, though they do seek to persuade and thus to be "a word on target," as J. C. Beker aptly puts it.[29]

Since all the letters are addressed to Christians, we must not make the mistake of thinking they represent a reproduction of Paul's missionary preaching, except where Paul alludes to such preaching. As letters, these documents, including Romans, are *not* intended to provide a compendium of Paul's thought or even all of his thoughts on any given subject.

Furthermore, these letters are neither examples of ivory-tower theologizing, nor rhetorical treatises composed as *purely* literary exercises. Paul uses rhetoric as a means to an end, not as an end in itself, and thus he uses it with some degree of flexibility as well as finesse. Paul was a pastor, and he writes for the purpose of meeting a specific need, dealing with a problem, or encouraging a congregation. Some letters are more geared to problem-solving and others are more oriented toward encouraging progress in the faith.[30] The letter to the Philippians seems to be basically the latter sort of document, not least because the letter does not end with an appeal to the stronger emotions, which was normal when the difficulties the orator or rhetorical writer was addressing were large (see 2 Corinthians). We must do our homework and ask how a given letter would have been understood and what the apostle intended for the audience to understand.[31]

B. Philippians as Rhetoric

Studying the rhetorical form of Paul's letters is a new discipline, and any results that we come up with will necessarily be tentative and subject to further correction. Nevertheless, the evidence that Paul has chosen to cast his letters in a rhetorical form, using rhetorical elements recognizable by his audience,[32] is considerable.[33] We must briefly chronicle the rhetorical climate in which Paul spoke.

Beginning in 14 C.E., rhetoric became the primary discipline in Roman higher education.[34] This was not simply a matter of reviving classical Aristotelian rhetoric, for now stress was placed on style and stylistic devices such as figures of speech, exclamations, apostrophes, and the like, all of which we find regularly in Paul's letters. Also stressed were word play and epigrams. While the ancients had seen rhetoric as chiefly the art of persuasion, by the time Quintilian wrote his masterpiece, the *Institutio Oratoria*, around 95 C.E., he was willing to say that rhetoric had become the art of *speaking well* (see *Inst. Or.* 2.15.1ff.). Paul is more interested in persuasion than mere ornamentation or simply speaking well. Nonetheless he does not neglect matters of style.

Greco-Roman rhetoric, however, was not just a matter of form; it was also a matter of content. In particular, it had to do with the narration of facts, proofs and refutations in order to persuade.[35] "The entire hope of victory and the entire method of persuasion rest on proof and refutation, for when we have submitted our arguments and destroyed those of the opposition, we have, of course, completely fulfilled the speaker's function" (*Rhetor. ad Heren.* 1.9.19).[36] Teachers of rhetoric such as Isocrates and later Quintilian regularly make remarks like the following:

> Therefore, I would have the orator, while careful in his choice of words, be even more concerned about his subject matter. For, as a rule, the best words are essentially suggested by the subject matter and are discovered by their own intrinsic light.... It is with a more virile spirit that we should pursue eloquence who, if only her whole body be sound, will never think it her duty to polish her nails and tie her hair. The usual result of over-attention to the

niceties of style is the deterioration of our eloquence. (*Inst. Or.* 8.Pr. 21–22)

There is thus both a formal and a material reason why Paul might use rhetoric. He wished to speak in a manner so that his audience would hear and heed his message. T. Engsberg-Pedersen explains,

> With regard to this, however, Paul has also shown that precisely when the question is one of changing other people's lives the very content of the gospel demands a "method" of effecting such changes which is directly opposed to any use of force.... It is that of speaking *to* them in ways that do not encroach upon their independence.[37]

In short, it requires the "art of persuasion," which involves exhortation and argument and only rarely commands.[38] The use of rhetoric was especially important in cities that had been and were being heavily influenced by Greco-Roman values, for example, in the city of Philippi, which was a Roman colony in Macedonia, having as its official name Colonia Iulia Augusta Philippensis.

The function of a good deal of rhetoric was to arouse the emotions, which were divided into *pathos* and *ethos*. The former included the stronger feelings such as anger, fear, and pity; the latter the gentler emotions such as the capacity for laughter. Quintilian tells us that humor includes: (1) speaking in such a way that one refutes, reproves, or generally makes light of an opponent's argument; (2) saying things that on the surface appear absurd or paradoxical; and (3) using words in a different sense than is usual (see *Inst. Or.* 6.2 and 6.3). Paul resorts to all these tactics, especially in 2 Corinthians, where he pulls out all the rhetorical stops, using even satire and irony.

Ethos has to do with the rhetor's character, which must be established at the outset; *logos* has to do with the arguments the rhetor will present in his speech or letter; and *pathos* is what the rhetor hopes to arouse in the audience. A speech or rhetorical letter usually attempts first to establish the speaker's *ethos* or character; second, to perform the act of persuasion or argumentation; and finally to present an emotional appeal to the audience to accept what has been said.[39] Paul's letters basically conform to this pattern of persuasion.

There are three primary species of rhetoric: forensic, deliberative, and epideictic. The first of these is concerned with accusations and defense, and thus focuses on the past. Deliberative rhetoric is more properly called the art of persuasion or dissuasion, and is mainly future-oriented. Finally, epideictic rhetoric is a matter of praising or blaming in order to encourage agreement with or rejection of some value, and usually focuses on the present.

In Philippians the primary task is to produce *concordia*, concord or unity in the congregation, and to that end Paul primarily uses deliberative rhetoric, though one may debate the species of rhetoric found in what is possibly a digression in chapter 3. Paul does not hesitate to use various species of persuasion to achieve his aims.[40]

The arrangement of a rhetorical piece usually breaks down into either four or six parts. The *exordium* is the beginning part, aimed at making the audience open and indeed well-disposed toward what follows. This is followed by the *narratio,* which explains to the audience the nature of the matters on which the discourse will dwell. Then comes the *partitio* or *propositio* (which is often included in the *narratio*), where the essential proposition(s) of the speaker and perhaps also of the opponent are laid out. The *probatio* brings in arguments to support the speaker's case, which is followed by the *refutatio* (often part of or included in the *probatio*), where the opponent's arguments are disproved or weakened. Finally, the *peroratio* recapitulates the main points of the *probatio,* attempting to arouse the emotions for the speaker's viewpoint by means of amplifying what has been said before.

One could mix different types of rhetoric in one document or speech in order to convey a point best.[41] This should not surprise us, for there were occasions where in the midst of urging a particular future course of action for a city, a rhetor might also have to defend himself and his own previous record.[42] For example, in the course of his defense speech on behalf of Marcellus, Cicero is also operating in a deliberative mode because he is implicitly, and at points almost explicitly, urging a future action — regicide![43] Later epistolary theorists, such as Libanius, recognized the "mixed" type of rhetorical letter,[44] and even among the church fathers, John Chrysostom saw in Galatians a mixture of two sorts of rhetoric.[45]

What primarily determines the character of a piece of rhetoric is not whether it has all of the elements of the standard textbook arrangement of a speech, for one or more of those elements were often omitted in actual speeches, though they all attend to the matters of *ethos, logos,* and *pathos,* but whether the *function* of the speech or letter is attempting mainly to persuade in regard to some future action, to defend some past course of action, or to offer praise or blame about something in the present. In this regard Philippians is clearly a deliberative piece of rhetoric, and it is far from artless or randomly arranged.

We will follow the normal procedure in studying a rhetorical document, whereby one looks for discrete rhetorical units marked by evidence of *inclusio,* a beginning and end of the unit. We will also be concerned with discerning the rhetorical situation of the document. By this is meant what persons, events, relationships, or other factors have prompted or necessitated this rhetorical composition. The urgent problem or imperfection that has prompted this response is called an *exigence.* Considerations of style, invention, and effectiveness of the rhetorical composition also come into play when one evaluates a piece of rhetoric.[46]

Rhetors were found in all of the great cities of the Roman Empire, especially in university towns like Tarsus and even in strongly Jewish cities like Jerusalem, which was under direct Roman rule from 6 C.E. Rhetoric was not seen in antiquity in the way we view elocution lessons or speech exercises today. Rather, since eloquence was one of the main cultural objectives, rhetoric was seen as "the crown and completion of any liberal education worthy of its name."[47] Since reading was always done aloud, the difference between reading and speaking was often slim, and thus "the categories of eloquence were imposed on every form of mental activity," including the writing of letters.[48] H. I. Marrou stresses that "Hellenistic culture was above all things of a rhetorical culture, and its typical literary form was the public lecture."[49] The same can be said of Greco-Roman culture.

It is a mistake to assume rhetoric was something only the well-to-do or well-educated practiced. As D. E. Aune says:

> The literary conventions and styles of the upper classes percolated down to lower levels, and they occur in attenuated and simplified forms in popular literature. For elevated literary forms and styles were not locked away in the libraries and salons of the rich and educated, they were on public display. During the first and second centuries A.D. public performances by rhetoricians were in great demand, and they (like contemporary movie stars or rock musicians) received wealth and prestige along with fame. . . . All levels of the population of the Roman world were exposed to the variety of structures and styles found in the rhetoric, literature, and art that were on public display throughout the Empire.[50]

In such an environment, letters in the hands of a Cicero or a Paul became extensions of oral speech and especially of dialogues. Thus, the rhetorical conventions of public speech and discourse were carried over into written documents such as letters. Rhetoric gave Paul a means to relate to and indeed impress his Philippian audience. Even those who had had little education would have heard speeches that followed the conventions of rhetoric and would have been able to appreciate much of Paul's artistry. Marrou reminds us:

> Rhetoric gave the ancients a system of formal values that supplied prose with its own aesthetic . . . a system, open to all educated people, and peacefully installed at the heart of a tradition which was passed down for centuries from generation to generation, [which] meant a common standard, a common denominator between all types of intelligence, uniting writers and public, the classics and the "moderns" in mutual understanding and harmony.[51]

The popularity of rhetoric during the period of the Roman Empire is not hard to document. Whether one considers the various important literary works that lionized orators during the Empire (e.g., Athenaeus, *Deipnosophists;* Philostratus, *Lives of the Sophists*), or the examples of orators who became wealthy by traveling through cities and declaiming their speeches, or orators who were wealthy and made major benefactions to various cities such as Corinth (e.g., Herodes Atticus), the evidence is plentiful that there was a great relish for oratory during this period.[52]

The art of persuasion, as it was originally used, and many felt was intended to be used, was the kind of art that best flourished in a democratic setting or in the midst of a voluntary society. Deliberative rhetoric was the stuff of the assembly when it freely debated the proper course for the *polis* to take, just as forensic rhetoric was the form used in the law court, and epideictic rhetoric was most often used in funeral oratory or public speeches when some person or thing was being lauded or lambasted.[53] What happened, however, when most of the remnants of democracy were snuffed out during the age of the Empire? In such a situation the rhetoric of flattery or pure polemics flourished while substantive or philosophical rhetoric fell on hard times. In the Empire, the rhetoric of pure display or ornamentation came to the fore.

Forensic oratory continued to have a "situation in life" in the law courts, and it is no accident that the handbooks of rhetoric such as that of Quintilian focused especially on forensic rhetoric. It was the major substantive form of rhetoric for the serious minded who wished to use rhetoric in daily life, and not simply at funerals or special ceremonies praising an emperor or in assemblies where, though there might be deliberative speeches, power usually dictated what would be concluded.[54] Roman law and its system of jurisprudence encouraged young men who wished to have public success to pay special attention to forensic rhetoric.[55]

That Paul used rhetoric with his converts indicates his commitment to the Christian community as a society that should be led by means of persuasion if possible, and commanded only when necessary. That Paul used deliberative rhetoric as well with the Philippian community suggests that he believed the Christian community there had a future and that it needed to make decisions pertaining to that future. It is no accident that Paul chose the term *ekklēsia* for the gathering together of his converts. This was the familiar term for a public assembly where in ancient times deliberative discourse was heard and debated. It was not a technical term for a religious gathering, much less a Christian one. Paul may have envisioned that the Christian assembly would become like other forums that nurtured freedom and worked by means of willing consent of the participants.

Probably he envisioned the reading of his Philippian letter in the Christian assembly as a surrogate for the deliberative discourse he would have delivered in person. If so, we might expect that some attention would be given in such letters to various *aural* devices, such as alliteration, meant to affect the ear and to aid persuasion.

The Empire, due to its very character, primarily encouraged or nurtured either forensic or epideictic rhetoric, though there were various occasions when deliberative rhetoric might be used, for instance, when an ambassador might try to convince his audience of the proper decision to make about some future course of action. Epedeictic rhetoric in many cases became quite banal, when an orator in public or a schoolboy declaimed on hypothetical or trivial subjects such as the praiseworthiness of a flea or the shameful baldness of a man's head.

Declamation, which at its best was a school exercise on a purely hypothetical topic in order to hone one's skills, became a form of public entertainment.[56] Rhetoric became an end in itself: mere ornamentation, elocution, and execution with an aim to please the crowd. This sort of rhetoric, without serious content or intent other than to play to and sway the crowd's emotions, was precisely the sort of nonthreatening, apolitical kind of rhetoric Roman society could encourage and enjoy. Paul was not interested in merely entertaining his audiences, however; he wished to persuade them. His rhetoric must be seen in the light of the way the more serious-minded, such as Isocrates, Cicero, or Quintilian, used rhetoric, not in the way declaimers or Sophists did so.

At this point we must present the rhetorical arrangement of the letter and discuss briefly the factors that caused Paul to produce such a document, arguing for *concordia* and being of "one mind."[57]

1. Epistolary prescript — 1:1-2;

2. Epistolary thanksgiving and *exordium* — 1:3-11;

3. Epistolary body introduced by the "I wish you to know" formula (cf. 2 Cor. 8:1; 1 Cor. 10:1), followed by a brief *narratio* explaining some of the situation or facts prompting the writing of the letter — 1:12-26;

4. The *propositio* offering the basic thesis statement of the discourse — 1:27-30;

5. The *probatio* — 2:1-4:3 (which often includes a *refutatio* if there are arguments of adversaries to deal with — see 3:2-21).

The *probatio* is the real essence of a rhetorical speech or letter, making up the principal arguments used to persuade the audience. It is possible for these arguments to be arranged according to certain topics, as is the case in 1 Corinthians, but here Paul is interested in presenting a variety of arguments, using positive and negative models or examples all dealing with one basic issue — what produces harmony, concord, unity in the Philippian congregation and between the Philippians and Paul. Paul chooses to deal with the most delicate matters at the end of the discourse, the first being the concrete example of disunity in Philippi caused by two leading female Christians there, Euodia and Syntyche (4:2-3). Extraordinarily, he reserves to the end of the *peroratio* the discussion of the even more delicate matter of "giving and receiving" that has gone on between Paul and the Philippians (4:10-20). This shows one of the main reasons for the writing of this document and the extreme caution and delicacy with which Paul approaches this financial matter, as is also the case when Paul addresses financial matters in some of his other letters (see 1 Cor. 9; 2 Cor. 8-9).[58]

The first full argument then comes in 2:1-18 and involves the appeal to Christ as an example of behavior that produces godly results of unity, concord, and the like.[59] Yet one must bear in mind that in the first chapter Paul has already appealed to his own positive example (1:12ff.). and also to the negative example of his rivals who proclaim the gospel out of selfish motives. This is followed by a second argument (2:19–3:1a), largely in narrative form, which implicitly appeals to Timothy and Epaphroditus, who are exemplary in being sons of the gospel and cooperative and diligent co-workers who fall in with Paul's designs. This is followed in turn by Paul's third argument in 3:1b–4:1, where he compares and contrasts himself with the "dogs" about whom he wishes to warn or remind the Philippians. The final part of the *probatio* comes with a brief fourth argument found in 4:2–3. Thus, in the argument section of the letter Paul appeals to positive and negative examples of behavior that produce peace, concord, unity: on the positive side, (1) Christ; (2) Timothy and Epaphroditus (and thus by implication most of the Philippians themselves since they sent him); and (3) Paul; and on the negative side (1) the "dogs"; (2) Euodia and Syntyche; and (3) this perverse generation (2:15).

    6. The *peroratio* — 4:4–20;

Here Paul reprises various arguments he has mentioned or alluded to earlier in the discourse and further develops one that is mentioned only in passing in the *exordium,* the matter of giving and receiving. The *peroratio* then would begin at 4:4ff. with a hortatory note, which is appropriate, and then continue with a second division at 4:10ff. The tone shows that the appeal to strong emotions or the use of *indignatio* was not necessary, since this is basically a deliberative progress-oriented letter, not a major problem-solving letter. Either the opposition is possible but not actual in Philippi, or it is not currently present in Philippi, or it is not major, the Philippians being basically loyal to Paul.

    7. Epistolary Greetings and Closing — 4:21–23.

Overall it appears to me that this letter is about positive and negative examples on which the Philippians must pattern themselves or which they must shun, and is thus a largely deliberative argument for *concordia.* These examples are surrounded by exhortations to follow or ignore them, and encouragements for the

Philippians to go on in a positive direction, being like-minded, striving for unity and harmony:

I. Positive and negative examples in chapter 1: (1) Paul (vv. 12–14; 18b–30); and (2) his rival preachers of the gospel in Rome (vv. 15–18a);

II. Positive and negative examples in chapter 2: (1) Christ (vv. 5–11); (2) this crooked and depraved generation (v. 15); and (3) implied positive examples, Timothy and Epaphroditus (vv. 19–30);

III. Positive and negative examples in chapter 3: (1) the Judaizers or dogs (vv. 2–6, 18–19) contrasted to (2) Paul (vv. 5–17, 20–21);

IV. Negative examples in chapter 4: in Philippi itself, Euodia and Syntyche (vv. 2–3).

The concluding *peroratio* includes a statement of the qualities one looks for in such examples, the Greco-Roman virtues (4:8–9).

Lest these observations about Paul's strategy seem novel to some, it should be pointed out that until the decline in the study of the classics by biblical scholars in the late nineteenth and early twentieth centuries, the rhetorical skills of Paul were widely recognized by most scholars ranging from John Chrysostom in the early church to J. Weiss at the end of the nineteenth century. Weiss, in his classic work *Beiträge zur Paulinischen Rhetorik,* shows how many passages in Philippians, not just the Christ hymn, reflect considerable skill in rhetorical composition.[60] This letter is far from artless prose lacking careful arrangement of form and content.

III. Roman Philippi and Paul's Philippian Audience

Though Philippi was originally a city built and fortified by Philip, the father of Alexander the Great, in 358–357 B.C.E., the Philippi that Paul knew was a Roman city, indeed a Roman colony, and so a metropolis run on the principles of Roman law, with Roman officials, ideology, and culture. Of course Roman citizenship was highly prized in such a place. Following the victory of the Roman army over the Persians in 168 B.C.E., Philippi became an important and strategic spot as one of the major stopping places on the Via Egnatia that connected Rome with the East. It was located in a very fertile region eight miles from the sea, and at various periods in its history gold was mined nearby.

The city was best known to the Romans from a historical point of view as the place where Brutus and Cassius, the infamous assassins of Julius Caesar, fought Marc Antony and Octavian in 42 B.C.E., with the latter prevailing. Eventually, when Octavian defeated Antony at Actium in 31 B.C.E., having taken the title Augustus, he rebuilt Philippi as a military outpost, populated it with Roman soldiers, made it a colony (see Acts 16:12), and even gave it the *ius italicum,* that is, the legal character of a Roman territory in Italy which was the very highest honor ever bestowed on a provincial city. In practical terms this meant that there would be no poll or land taxes in Philippi, and colonists could purchase, own, or transfer property plus engage in civil law suits. The city was made a senatorial province in 27 B.C.E. by Augustus, was transferred by Tiberius to his own personal control as an imperial province in 15 C.E., and then was transferred back to the senate's control by Claudius in 44 C.E. The proconsul who governed the province had his administrative seat in Thessalonica, not in Philippi. In any case Philippi's links with Rome were numerous and strong, and there was regular social interchange between the two cities aided by imperial slaves or freedmen acting as couriers between Rome and the East (see Phil. 4:22).[61]

Indeed Philippi was in many ways Rome in microcosm and chiefly populated by Romans, though there were also some Greeks and apparently a few Jews as well. Acts 16:11ff. suggests that Paul could find no synagogue within the Philippian walls, and this comports with other evidence that the Jewish population in this city was not large.[62] This same account also suggests that women soon came to play a prominent role in the fledgling Christian community at Philippi, something Philippians 4:2–3 only confirms.[63] This is not surprising in view of the variety of roles women assumed in Macedonian society in general since at least the Hellenistic era.[64] For example, R. MacMullen points to a woman who was a high priestess in Macedonia.[65]

If we ask about the social makeup of Paul's audience in Philippi several things may be affirmed. First, it is likely that the majority of Paul's audience was one or another sort of Gentile,[66] and in the main their cultural orientation would have been Greco-Roman with an emphasis on the last half of that hyphenated word. The few names mentioned in Philippians as associated with the church there may suggest converts with some Greek background, but we cannot be sure.[67] Having said this, there is nothing improbable with the suggestion, prompted by Acts 16, that some of the first converts may have been Gentile adherents to the Jewish religion. This may in part explain the reason for the warnings in Philippians 3. The character of the letter itself, which in many ways has the least Jewish flavor of all his epistles, also favors the conclusion that the majority of the audience is Gentile.

Second, not only the generosity of the Macedonians but also their poverty is suggested in 2 Corinthians 8–9 and 11:9, and at least the former is suggested of the Philippians in chapter 4. We may suspect that as in Paul's other congregations, particularly in Corinth, there were Christians of various socio-economic standings in Philippi. This is suggested not only by Acts 16, which refers to a rather well-to-do woman and her servants,[68] but also by various hints in Philippians that we will discuss in the commentary itself. What is not suggested in Philippians is the sort of serious social tensions created by the social differences we find in 1 Corinthians. The letter also suggests that there were capable women and men assuming leadership roles in and for the Philippian congregation. This leads to some further considerations of other social matters.

IV. Social Concerns

Though we will reserve the detailed discussion of social matters until we get to the text, here we will introduce the reader to some of the important issues raised by Philippians for social historians. First, there is the matter of social networks.[69] One must explore the networks that existed between Paul, his co-workers, and his audience to understand the nature and functions of their relationships. Especially in view of the colony status of Philippi and thus its close connections with Rome, one must also consider the imperial networks of power, especially in regard to the vexed question of the household of Caesar.[70] One must ask why the saints who belong to Caesar's household especially send the Philippians greetings. Why also the boast about the Praetorium in 1:13?

A second major social issue, helpfully addressed by G. Peterman, is the issue of Paul's monetary relationships with the Philippians vis-à-vis the sort of relationships he had with others.[71] Should this relationship be seen as a *societas* relationship, a sort of limited partnership, as J. Paul Sampley suggests,[72] or would it be better to see it as being like other types of "friendship" (*amicitia*) relationships involving "giving and receiving." This issue is complex. We must determine whether some sort of patronage is involved and, if so, what that might imply about Paul's relationship with the Philippians, or whether their aid may be more simply characterized as missionary support or even missionary relief aid.[73]

A third issue, which Paul himself raises, is that of Roman citizenship vis-à-vis heavenly citizenship. How should Paul and the Philippians value and evaluate such citizenships; which sort mattered the most and how should that affect one's day-to-day life? Was Paul in a place and position where his Roman citizenship might matter a great deal? Is the appeal to the Greco-Roman virtues in chapter 4 telling about the character of the audience?

There is also the question of the social structures within the Philippian church: Who were the *episkopoi* and *diakonoi?* Why must Paul correct Euodia and Syntyche in a congregational letter meant to be read in worship? What exactly was Epaphroditus's role in Philippi?

The state of the system of Roman jurisprudence and what light it sheds on Philippians and Paul's actual condition and status need to be reflected on as well. On what basis might Paul have hopes, legally speaking, to be released in the not too distant future? Does this have any bearing on the probable location from which this letter was written? What do we know about provincial citizens appealing to Caesar and bypassing provincial justice systems?[74] These sorts of issues and questions should be kept in mind as we read the commentary.

V. Authorship, Date, Occasion, Unity, Opponents of Philippians

About the Pauline authorship of Philippians there is little or no debate, and thus we must turn our attention to more controverted matters. According to Acts (see 15:39–18:22), Paul first visited Philippi on his second missionary tour, probably around 50–51 C.E., and returned there again on several occasions, including on his way to Jerusalem near the end of his third missionary journey, perhaps as late as 57 C.E. (see 20:5). If Acts is to be believed, and the indication of a considerable lapse of time is taken seriously in Philippians 4:10–20, this would suggest that Philippians was written either sometime between the second and third missionary journeys, during some sort of incarceration or, much more likely, sometime after the third missionary journey perhaps during the Caesarean imprisonment in the late 50s (58–59?) or the house arrest in Rome (60–62).

It has been suggested that this letter was written during an Ephesian imprisonment, but this idea faces serious difficulties for the following reasons. First, neither Paul's letters nor Acts suggests such an imprisonment and certainly not one of the duration indicated by Philippians itself. Both 1 Corinthians 15:32 and 2 Corinthians 1:8 speak metaphorically and literally of afflictions and suffering but not of confinement in Ephesus and the province of Asia. Second, the notion of an Ephesian imprisonment is usually coupled with conjectures about an early date for Philippians, yet several important factors count against this.

The letter itself suggests a significant lapse of time since Paul received help from the Philippians, and an even longer period since "the beginning of the gospel" in Philippi. Furthermore, one extremely crucial theme that has direct bearing on the Philippians, the Collection, is never mentioned in Paul's letter to them, yet in 2 Corinthians 8–9 Paul brags that they made a generous contribution. In view of the references to the Collection in Galatians, 1 and 2 Corinthians, and Romans, it is hard to believe that Paul would make no reference to it if Philippians were a letter written in the same general period as these letters and either before or just after the Collection was delivered to Jerusalem. If, on the other hand, a considerable period of time has elapsed since the Collection had been delivered *and since the congregations who participated in it had been notified of its successful delivery*, the lack of reference to it in Philippians is not strange. The attempt of D. Georgi to see in Philippians 4:10–23 a reference to the Collection fails, for he overlooks the character of the passage and technical financial language used in that passage. Paul is referring to a relationship of "giving and receiving" between himself and the Philippians that he has only with the Philippians, not a Collection for the saints in Jerusalem.[75]

The dating of Philippians hinges on the question of Paul's location when he wrote this letter, and so we must address this matter carefully by considering the two major options — Caesarea Maritima and Rome. Let it first be said that while the distance factor has led some to consider Ephesus a possible locale for Paul's captivity, distance provides no advantage for Caesarea over Rome. The trip between Philippi and Rome would normally take between four and seven weeks, covering some 740 miles, and the time could be cut almost in half by imperial couriers who traveled by horse and/or carriage.[76] The distance, regardless of means of travel, is even farther from Philippi to Caesarea than to Rome. I would suggest that the distance factor has been overrated in the discussion, especially if, as seems likely, Epaphroditus became ill while he was on the way to visit Paul, and the Philippians first heard of it from other Christians heading east rather than from Paul.

On first blush, the reference to the Praetorium in Acts 23:35 might seem to favor the Caesarea locale, but several factors weaken this point. While it is true enough that a Roman governor's residence could be called a Praetorium in the provinces, when Paul boasts that his witness has gone out "throughout the whole Praetorium" in Philippians 1:13, this would hardly be much of a boast in Caesarea. But if Paul means his witness had been heard by the whole Praetorian guard in Rome, then the phrasing used has a certain suitability. It is more natural in any case to take the phrase about the Praetorium to refer to people and not a place, since it is joined with the clearly personal phrase "and to all the rest."

Second, it is not convincing to argue that Paul's life was in any serious danger *while* he was sequestered and guarded in Caesarea, and yet this seems clearly to be the case when he writes to the Philippians. His ability to appeal to Caesar while in Caesarea, as Acts says he finally does, also makes Caesarea a less likely place of origin for this letter.

Third, while Paul's having already made a first defense, according to Philippians 1, comports with the various stages recorded about the Caesarean imprisonment, it also comports with the normal procedure Paul would have faced in Rome, where he would have appeared before the emperor or judge for an initial hearing before the case was resolved. Furthermore, nothing in Philippians clearly suggests Paul is incarcerated. The evidence as it stands can as easily refer to house arrest, with Paul possibly chained to a Roman soldier. Indeed, the reference to greetings from the brothers who are *with* Paul (Phil. 4:21–22) more naturally describes the scene we read of in Acts 28 than the one recorded in Acts 23. The reference to the household of Caesar, probably alluding to the imperial slaves and/or freedmen, is also most naturally taken to refer to what Paul would have encountered in Rome. This is so because they greet the Philippians. I would suggest that this alludes to the social network between Rome and its colonies, in this case in Philippi. Some of the Christian imperial slaves are known to the Philippian Christians likely because they had gone back and forth to Philippi, perhaps as couriers on previous occasions. I thus agree with Lightfoot, Silva, O'Brien, Bruce, and others that Rome is the most likely site from which this letter was written.[77] All of these considerations lead me to date this letter somewhere toward the end of Paul's house arrest in Rome, perhaps about 62 C.E.

The issue of the occasion that prompted the writing of this letter can be dealt with more briefly. It is clear that Paul wants the Philippians to know of his status of his joy over their support, as the first and last chapters make clear. It is also evident that this letter is prompted because Paul is concerned about the disintegrating unity in Philippi, perhaps caused by both internal and external factors. Philippians 3 may suggest that Paul thought the Philippians might have to deal with Judaizers in the near future, if they were not already doing so (see below), and 4:2-3 makes evident that there were internal sources of disunity. Philippians 2:25ff. does not intimate that Paul is writing to inform the Philippians for the first time that Epaphroditus is ill, but it is part of his purpose to explain why he is sending him back. Possibly the Philippians had sent him along to be an ongoing aid to Paul, and Paul must not appear to be rejecting their gift, either the personal one or the money that came with Epaphroditus. These were delicate matters.

We have already presented our discussion of the rhetorical structure of the letter, but now it is necessary to discuss further the matter of its unity. It has often been thought that at least Philippians 3:2-21 and possibly also 4:10-20 are fragments of separate letters. The transition from Philippians 3:1 to 3:2 is seen as especially abrupt, reflecting an awkward attempt to blend two sources together, especially when, if one leaves 3:2-21 out, the transition from 3:1 to 4:1 seems smooth to many.

There are, however, serious problems with these arguments. First, there is not a shred of textual evidence that the two offending portions were ever absent from the letter to the Philippians. There is no textual evidence for interpolation, displacement, or multiple placement of either of these texts. Second, as W. J. Dalton and S. E. Fowl show, 3:20-21 recalls, develops, and applies the material in the Christ hymn in 2:6-11.[78] Third, 4:10-20, as D. F. Watson shows, is already alluded to in the *exordium* at 1:4-5 and at 2:25.[79] Fourth, Paul's letters are full of sudden shifts of tone and direction, and evidence of such is insufficient to force the conclusion that one is dealing with an interpolation. Fifth, as R. Jewett and D. Garland demonstrate, the letter has a good deal of special vocabulary and several key themes (such as the stress on oneness and being of one mind) that unite the four chapters, including the two debated portions.[80] Sixth, those who wish to argue for 3:2–21 being an interpolation must provide a plausible explanation why it was inserted, apparently so abruptly, just where it is. There is also no unanimity on where this supposed insertion begins and ends (beginning at 3:1b or 3:2? ending at 3:21 or 4:1?). Thus, quite apart from the argument for the rhetorical unity for the letter, which we will sustain throughout the commentary, there are strong indicators that all of Philippians should be considered part of one document.

Our last major subject concerns the "opponents" that Paul discusses in this letter. Recent work on the subject of Paul's opponents by G. Lyons and J. L. Sumney has rightly urged caution in the use of "mirror-reading" in the reconstruction of the existence and views of Paul's opponents.[81] By mirror-reading I mean that when Paul makes an assertion, even a strong one, one cannot assume an equal and opposite view is held by someone thus prompting Paul's words. This observation is all the more important in light of Paul's use of rhetoric where sometimes he is *forestalling* possible problems from arising and not dealing with actual current difficulties or adversaries. This technique is to be expected in deliberative rhetoric, which is inherently future-oriented.

The question then remains, what are we to make of Philippians 1:15–17 and 3:2–3, 18–19? It is possible that the former text foreshadows and prepares for the discussion of the "dogs" in the latter.[82] At the very least both texts refer to preachers who are rivals to Paul, and Paul assumes his audience needs some warning or guidance about them. I think that on closer inspection the two texts, while both referring to rivals, are not referring to the same rivals. In Philippians 1:15–17 Paul discusses those who proclaim the true gospel but with doubtful motives. He does not fault the content of their preaching. The text also suggests that these rivals are in Rome, are taking advantage of Paul's current limited mobility to preach, and are bringing him grief while he is under house arrest.

By contrast Paul calls those discussed in 3:2ff. "dogs" and enemies of the cross of Christ. It is quite unnecessary to posit two groups under discussion in chapter 3. The telling remark, "their god is their belly, their glory their shame" (3:19), can be seen as a euphemistic way to refer to the fact that the opponents are ruled by and tout Jewish food laws and a concern for circumcision (see 3:2–3). There is no need to posit a separate libertine group alluded to in 3:19.

The passage begins in 3:2 with the verb *blepete*, which could mean simply "consider," in which case Paul is just offering an example that his audience is encouraged to shun, by contrast to Paul's own example, which they are to follow.[83] Even if, as most think, the verb means "beware," it is by no means clear that Paul thinks this group is currently in Philippi. He says two things that suggest that this warning or example has been referred to before in writing or speaking to this same audience: (1) he speaks of writing the same things over again (3:1b); and (2) he says he has often told them about these enemies of the cross of Christ (3:18). I conclude that Paul is referring to Judaizers, Torah-centric Jewish Christians such as those his Galatian converts encountered, but this looks like something of a reminder and/or forewarning about a perennial problem rather than an attack on a group currently troubling the Philippians. This would explain why Paul does not return to this topic in his final exhortations in the *peroratio*, which has a rather mild tone.

With these things in mind we turn now to the discussion of the text of Philippians itself. We will discuss each section of the letter according to its discrete rhetorical parts and will provide our own translation in the process.

Chapter Two

Epistolary Prescript — 1:1–2

Translation

1:1 Paul and Timothy, slaves of Christ Jesus, to all the saints in Christ Jesus who are in Philippi with the overseers and deacons. **2**Grace to you and peace from God our Father and the Lord Jesus Christ.

Paul, in this letter as in others, uses the letter-writing conventions of his day and so the addresser(s) are mentioned first, then the addressee, followed by the initial greeting to the addressee. We will examine the salutation first. It was common practice among Diaspora Jews to take Greek names that were close in sound to their Jewish names, as did Paul, whose Hebrew name is Saul.[1] It is worth pointing out that Acts does not suggest that Paul's name change came as a result of his conversion, but rather as a result of his missionary work, coming as it did when he began to reach out to the Gentiles (see Acts 13:6–12). This is not the only letter where Timothy is mentioned with Paul in the superscript (see 1 Thess. 1:1; 2 Thess. 1:1; Phlm. v. 1). It does not appear, however, that Timothy co-wrote the letter, for Paul goes on to use "I" throughout and distinguishes himself from Timothy as someone whom he will send at 2:19.

In any event, Paul calls them both *douloi.* It is not clear whether the primary background for this usage is the OT, which speaks of leaders being in a special sense God's servants, or the Greek, for the term literally means "slaves." If Philippians 2, where Christ is called a *doulos* in the Christ-hymn, is any clue, the OT background may be to the fore and Paul may be think-

30

ing of the example of Moses or Joshua, and/or the servant in Isaiah 53 may be in view.[2] Yet it is hard to avoid the conclusion that a largely Gentile congregation would have heard this term as suggesting primarily that the person in question is the slave of Christ, his property. Paul certainly believed that he owed his allegiance to Christ as his master and Lord (both terms used for slave owners in antiquity).

In the first verse we also hear something about the leadership structure or function that existed in Philippi: it requires *episkopoi* (plural) and *diakonoi* (plural). It may well be true that these terms are not yet technical terms for bishops and deacons, but they do indicate some kind of leadership structure that involves various people and a differentiation between two sorts of leadership roles. The etymology of the former term suggests that what is meant by *episkopoi* is overseers, those who watch over and care for the congregation. The term *diakonoi* is rightly taken to refer to some sort of practical service (the term originally meant literally "one who waits on tables"). Perhaps the leaders are mentioned at the outset because Paul is expecting them to set an example of unitive behavior for the congregation in Philippi and perhaps also to resolve the conflict referred to in 4:2–3. Another possibility is that they are mentioned because they specially commissioned Epaphroditus to bring the gift to Paul, and Paul must recognize them.[3] Alternately, it is possible they are mentioned because they were not acting in humility but rather were exalting themselves, and so by contrast Paul shames them by avoiding the use of the term "apostle" here and calling himself a "slave."[4] This would be part of his rhetorical strategy to produce unity and concord in Philippi despite squabbles in the leadership (see below on 4:2–3).[5]

One of the major flaws in L. G. Bloomquist's rhetorical discussion of Philippians is that he assumes too much about Paul's social situation at the time he is writing. In the first place it cannot be assumed that Paul is imprisoned or that he is presently physically suffering due to incarceration. It appears that he is under some sort of house arrest, whether in his own dwelling or in some accessible place like the Praetorium. I would suggest the former. Nor can we assume that the term *doulos* has anything to do with his captivity, since in all the other places Paul uses this term he is not a captive (see Rom. 1:1; Gal. 1:10; 2 Cor. 4:5). Philippians actually suggests that Paul has considerable access to friends and colleagues, even those with gifts, and the main suffering Paul seems to be undergoing *at present* is his chafing at the bit to be free, or at least to have his case resolved one way or another so that he can get on with ministry unfettered, or alternately go and be with the Lord.[6] While the Philippians in their sending of an emissary with a gift may have assumed Paul is in dire straits, one of the functions of this letter is to allay such fears on their part.[7] It is important at this point to say something about the leadership structures of the Pauline churches.

A Closer Look: The Networks of Power

One of the more frequently promulgated half-truths about the early Christian church is that it began with a pneumatic or charismatic form of leadership and evolved into an institutionalized (and patriarchal) form of church governance. At least in regard to the Pauline communities the reality was considerably more complex. Several factors affected the structure of the Pauline communities, including both spiritual gifts and social factors. For example, those who were able to house the early Christian meetings seem to have assumed the responsibility not only for providing a venue for the meeting but also for structuring how the meeting would proceed, or at least deciding when there would be a meeting with a meal in the context of which the Lord's Supper was shared (see 1 Cor. 11:17ff.).[8]

There seems in fact to have been a three-tiered structure of leadership in the Pauline communities, with apostles at the top, then the Pauline co-workers, such as Timothy, who also were itinerant, and then the local leadership in the house church, which arose due to a variety of factors including those mentioned above. There was then a hierarchy of power and authority from the outset of these communities, but it was not a ethnically, socially, or gender-determined hierarchy, though these factors *affected* the structure in some respects. B. Holmberg insightfully suggests,

> There are sociological reasons for the relative insignificance of local offices too. One of them is the fact that this "office structure" has developed before the eyes of all concerned . . . [see 1 Cor 16:15-16]. The decisive reason is, however, the personage of Paul

himself. The founder has not left the scene, but is fully and energetically active in his churches (especially in Corinth). His letters show that he had full control over the life and development of his churches and regarded himself as having a permanent responsibility for them. Even if he aimed at fostering maturity and independence in his churches, his letters do not give the impression that he gave them the reins. And it is just this "potential accessibility" of the apostle ... that prevents the full (social, legal, and theological) developments of those beginnings of an office structure."[9]

What happens, however, when Paul has been long apart from his converts in Philippi and is currently incapable of visiting them? I would suggest that we see the results of such conditions in Philippians 1:1: there are local *episkopoi* and *diakonoi* whom Paul needs to recognize and greet. In other words, it is not true to say that local leadership developed only after Paul died. More likely it developed, was nurtured, and became more and more fully functional the further the distance in time or space the apostle was from his converts. Another consideration that may affect the discussion of the Philippian church's structure is that, unlike the church in Corinth, in Philippi Paul's authority seems to have been unquestioned by the converts. It is surely not accidental that Paul does not mention his apostolic status at the outset of Philippians: he assumes that his authority is unquestioned by these converts.[10] One must also not forget that Paul's co-workers assumed a wide variety of authorized tasks and often acted as Paul's surrogates.[11] This seems to have been the case with Timothy, who apparently played a role in the Philippian congregation from the very beginning (Acts 16:1–15) and had an active concern for them (Phil. 2:19–20). In view of the fact that the rest of this letter is written in the first person singular, we cannot assume Timothy is mentioned at the outset because he helped compose this letter. Rather, it is because he is a key link with the Philippians.[12]

Finally, what we may learn from the use of the terms *episkopoi* and *diakonoi* is that Paul's vision of Christian leadership is both servant leadership and oversight of the congregation. In view of the basic meanings of these terms one would expect the latter to refer to some sort of practical service and the former to some kind of overseeing. Perhaps the latter would be seen as subordinate to the former, but we cannot be sure. What is more certain is that since they are mentioned separately from the rest of the converts in Philippi they must have had some sort of ongoing official status. Perhaps such structures fully emerged only toward the close of Paul's ministry.

Often noted is the fact that Paul has modified the standard Greek greeting, which involved the word *chairein*, choosing instead its cognate *charis* (grace), and to this he adds the traditional Jewish word for greeting, "peace" (*shalom*). This may reflect Paul's mixed audience not only here but elsewhere since it is his most common form of greeting (Rom. 1:7; 1 Cor. 1:3; 2 Cor. 1:2; Gal. 1:3; Col. 1:2; 1 Thess. 1:1; 2 Thess. 1:2; Phlm. v. 3). As Hawthorne points out, by formulating things in this way an ordinary salutation is elevated to a blessing.[13] It is not just Paul who greets them, however, but God the Father and Jesus; they are the ultimate source of this grace and peace. This leads to the thanksgiving prayer or *exordium*.

Chapter Three

Exordium and Thanksgiving Prayer — 1:3–11

The Joy of Shared Faith and Ministry

The *exordium* in deliberative Greco-Roman rhetoric serves the purpose of setting forth or alluding in advance to the subjects to be addressed in the discourse, thus expressing at least some of the reasons for writing or speaking. There were two basic ways to approach the *exordium*. If one was addressing a hostile or indifferent audience, one would need to insinuate (*insinuatio*) the subject matter, all the while trying to ingratiate oneself with that audience (see Cicero *Inv.* 1.15–17; Quintilian *Inst. Or.* 4.1.42–51). This is clearly not the state of affairs between Paul and the Philippians, and so he is able to take the more direct tack of appealing to subjects that both he and the Philippians agree are worthy of attention and honorable (see Phil. 1:10 and 4:8–9). Paul's moral character is not at issue in this letter, and thus he may hold up himself and others as examples the Philippians should follow. Paul is able to appeal directly to the audience's goodwill and interests they share with the apostle (the common affection they share for each other, the common cause of the gospel). The appeal to the Philippians as Paul's partners in the gospel is an effective means of establishing goodwill.

While commentators have often noted that Paul introduces his subjects in the thanksgiving prayer and tries to establish a positive basis for the discussion that follows, they have often failed to realize why he does so. It is because, as a good rhetor, Paul must first establish *ethos*, positive feelings between himself and his audience, before he can address them, and the proper procedure in an *exordium* is to introduce the subjects to be discussed while establishing that *ethos*. The following is but a partial list of themes and key terms that are introduced in the *exordium* and recur later in the discourse:

1. joy-rejoice (1:4; cf. 1:18, 25; 2:2, 17, 18, 28, 29; 3:1; 4:1, 4, 10);

2. *koinōnia,* sharing (1:5, 7; cf. 2:1; 3:10; 4:14-15);

3. the gospel and its defense (1:5, 7; cf. 1:12, 16, 27; 2:22; 4:3, 15);

4. being convinced (1:6; cf. 1:14, 25; 2:24; 3:3);

5. think, be intent on (1:7; cf. 2:2, 5; 3:15, 19; 4:2, 10);

6. affection or love (1:8-9; cf. 1:16, 2:1-2, 12; 4:1);

7. being in Christ (1:1, 13; cf. 1:26; 2:1, 5; 3:14; 4:7, 19, 21);

8. the day of Christ (1:6, 10; cf. 2:16; 3:10-11, 20-21);

9. the Philippians' gift (1:3, 5; cf. 2:26, 4:10-20);

10. the stress on "any" and "all," which is part of the appeal for unity and concord in this letter (1:2, 4, 7, 8; cf. 2:1, 17; 4:21 and passim).[1]

As J. B. Lightfoot long ago noted, it is impossible not to connect the repeated use of the word "all" with Paul's strong exhortations to unity in this letter (1:27; 2:1-4; 4:2-9).[2] Paul is modeling behavior that produces unity by making clear that he prays for all and is concerned about the eternal well-being of all the converts in Philippi. "The three main functions of the exordium, to obtain audience attention, receptivity, and goodwill, are all performed by the *exordium* of Philippians."[3]

Translation

1:3I give thanks to my God for your every remembrance of me, **4**always in all my petitions for all of you with joy **5**making the petition, about your sharing in the [support of] the gospel from the first day until now, **6**confident in this itself — that the one who began in you a good work will complete it by the day of Christ Jesus. **7**Just as it is right for me to think of you all in this way, because you have me in your heart, in my bonds and in the defense and confirmation of the gospel all of you have been my fellow-sharers of grace. **8**For God is my witness how I long for all of you in the innermost being of Christ Jesus. **9**And this I pray, in order that your love might increase still more and more, in knowledge and in all insight for your distinguishing the superior, **10**in order that you may be pure and blameless on the Day of Christ, **11**filled with the fruit of righteousness, that [which comes] through Jesus Christ unto the glory and praise of God.

The prayers in Paul's letters often set the tone for what follows and frequently provide a preview of coming attractions, a hint of Paul's concerns and interests in the letter. This thanksgiving prayer is no different. One then should note the exceedingly positive tone of the prayer: we have terms like "joy," "confidence," "grace," "insight," bearing fruit. Paul also stresses the intimate connection between himself and the believers in Philippi with the term *koinōnia*. The term's most basic meaning is "have (something) in common with" and in a derived sense can mean "share in common with." *Koinōnia* is a relational word; it is not something one could call a room but rather must involve persons in relationship and something they have or share in common.[4] In view of the fact that elsewhere in Paul and the NT this same construction with *koinōnia* plus a phrase introduced by *eis* has the meaning of contributions, almsgiving, or, in other words, financial sharing, it is quite plausible that it primarily has that sense here (see 2 Cor. 9:13; Rom. 15:26; 2 Cor. 8:3-4; Phlm. v. 6; Heb. 13:16). Paul is grateful for the Philippians' generous sharing in the gospel ministry ever since he first presented them with the message. Paul then is already thinking of the generosity of the Philippians, for they have repeatedly shared in the gospel by financially aiding Paul (see 1 Thess. 4:16; 2 Cor. 11:9).

Thus Paul is alluding to what he will speak more openly about in 4:10ff.

This conclusion is strongly supported by the recent work of G. Peterman demonstrating the numerous verbal and content parallels between this *exordium* in 1:3-11 and 4:10-20 (note the shared references to thanksgiving, joy, *koinōnia*, the gospel, "from the beginning" (1:5) compared to "in the beginning" (4:15), thinking and thoughtfulness of each other, partnership, fruit, and God's glory).[5] The reference to the gift in the term *koinōnia* also makes it likely that the very first clause of the prayer refers to this matter as well and should be translated "for your every remembrance of me," not Paul's remembrance of them. It is they who have remembered him once again financially as they had regularly done in the past, and Paul is thankful and rejoicing because of it.[6]

Verse 6 seems to refer to the process of internal sanctification, i.e., the work of God in the believers, the process of salvation that will not be completed until the day they see Christ face to face and have a resurrection body like Christ's. Only then, in Paul's view, will the physical, moral, and spiritual maturation process be finished. What Paul has done in this verse is shift the attention from the Philippians' good work to God's good work in and for them that is still in process of realization. The connection between vv. 5 and 6 is that the Philippians' generous giving is clear evidence that God is working in them to will and to do.

Verse 7 is ambiguous, but in view of what follows in v. 8, I take it to mean that Paul is saying, "you have me in your heart," as is shown by their gift, and not vice versa (though that is also true). Verse 7, using juridical terms, also refers to Paul's defense and confirmation of the gospel, and here quite likely he is referring to his *apologia* in a Roman court.[7] This would have happened during the initial meeting between Paul, the judge, and Paul's accusers (and advocates?) following the Roman procedure known as *cognitio*. The facts would be agreed upon and the basis for the judgment, the so-called *formula*, would be determined.[8] "It would seem that under Nero the necessary personal jurisdiction of the emperor, such as the trial of capital cases on appeal, was delegated to other persons, and the sentences confirmed by him afterwards."[9] It was the job of the Praetorian guard to take charge of prisoners sent from the provinces while they awaited trial or the final verdict.[10]

Verse 8 starts with a strong oath indicating how much Paul longs to see and be with what might be called his favorite congregation: "he longs for all of them in the entrails of Christ." As Hawthorne points out, the term *splanchna* means the nobler organs — heart, liver, lungs — and not the intestines, which are usually referred to by the Greek word *entera*.[11] The point is to indicate the depth of feeling both he and Christ have for them; in Paul's view they are in the very heart of Christ!

Verse 9 is significant on several accounts. As M. Silva has shown, there are various substantive parallels between this prayer and the one in Colossians 1:9-11, both referring to prayer, growing in knowledge, gaining discernment, being filled, bearing fruit, good works, and God's glory.[12] This suggests that this prayer was not spontaneously composed; it reflects rhetorical skill, using among other devices synonymous parallelism.[13] Verses 9ff. suggest that Paul does not think love without insight and moral discernment is adequate. Love without insight leads to spoiling and mere indulgence. It leads to bad moral judgments due to affection for someone. Insight and the ability to distinguish what is superior without love are also less than ideal. Paul wants their love to increase more and more in these qualities of discernment and knowledge. Then they will truly know how to love practically, how to decide when and how best to express that love.

There is some question as to whether *aproskopoi* (v. 10) means "blameless" or, in the more active sense, "harmless" (not stumbling and not causing others to stumble). It would seem that the term "pure" would lead one to expect "blameless." It is God who will fill them with the fruit of righteousness that comes through Christ and brings glory to God (v. 11).

Five major themes run through the *exordium:* (1) the Philippians' gift and ongoing participation in Paul's ministry; (2) God's work in them not only prompting such a gift, but also sanctifying them and helping them progress toward the ultimate goal of conformity to the image of Christ on the day he returns; (3) this work of God in them also giving them discernment and the right attitude to know what is good and what makes for the sort of behavior that pleases God and helps the community of Christ be one; (4) the great mutual affection that exists between Paul and the Philippians, which prompts the great concern of each for the other when they suffer; and (5) Paul's defense of the gospel and his ministry, even while in chains.

A careful examination will show that these themes recur at various points throughout the letter and are brought up in order to promote the overall goal of this piece of rhetoric, namely, to produce unity and the sort of behavior that leads to unity in the Philippian congregation by means of setting forth positive and negative examples of such behavior. Thus, the subject first mentioned in the prayer, the financial gift, Paul reserves for discussion last in the letter, for it is the most delicate matter (4:10–20). The subject of Paul's defense and presentation of the gospel is discussed more fully in the *narratio* that follows immediately in 1:12–26. The proper unitive judgment, character, and witness of the Philippians, comes up repeatedly and can be seen as the main subject of the discourse, as the *propositio* demonstrates in 1:27–30 (as does 2:1–5a, 12–18, 3:1ff. 15–16; 4:1–3), and the *peroratio* in 4:4–9. The subject of God's work for them and for Paul comes up in the hymn in 2:6–11, 3:10–14, 20–21. The theme of mutual affection and sharing is especially prominent in both the *exordium* and the final argument in 4:10–20, but it may also be seen in Paul's reference to his own travel plans and the sending of co-workers to them in his stead (see 2:19–30).

R. Jewett rightly stresses that the motif,

> of the correct mental attitude...is so important in Philippians that one wonders why exegetes have not paid much attention to it.... The word *phroneō* appears in these four short chapters a total of ten times, while appearing in the rest of the letters only eleven times. This theme links each section of the letter into one connected whole, beginning with a reference to Paul's attitude toward the Philippians (1:7), gaining its theological definition in the hymn to Christ (2:2, 3, 5), then being applied as a norm in the

discussion of the "gnostic" attitude (3:1, 5, 19) and in the discussion of the strife in the congregation (4:2). Finally it is used in regard to the Philippians' attitude toward Paul expressed in the offering (4:10).[14]

Paul has much to be thankful for in this letter in regard to what the Philippians have done and what God has done, is doing, and will do. Though there are still disuniting and disconcerting things that have to be overcome in Philippi, Paul exudes confidence and at various points expresses not only hope but confidence about how things will turn out both for himself and his converts. This is more of a progress-oriented than a problem-solving letter, and there is no indication Paul is responding to inquiries about difficulties that the Philippians had raised in a letter to the apostle, as is the case in 1 Corinthians.

Chapter Four _____

The *Narratio* — 1:12–26
ARRESTED DEVELOPMENT

A *narratio,* or narration of facts, is not always necessary in a deliberative piece of rhetoric, for the object of deliberative rhetoric is not to prove some set of facts true or false, but to argue for some future course of action as honorable, worthy, virtuous, and the like. Nevertheless, a narration of facts is in order in a deliberative piece of rhetoric if it helps remove an exigency or obstacle that exists between the orator and his audience so that he may persuade them and if it is pertinent to the situation the rhetor is addressing. In the case of Philippians it was necessary for Paul to relate to his audience what had happened and was happening to him, what difficulties he and the gospel were now facing, in order for him not only to allay his audience's concerns and fears,[1] but more importantly to provide them with an example of how to behave in the face of adversities and adversaries, both of which the Philippians were facing or might soon face.[2] In other words, the *narratio* serves the larger purpose of the discourse, which is to provide examples of behavior that make for unity and concord in the body of Christ.

As M. M. Mitchell says, "Although narrative is not always required in deliberative argumentation, we do find it to set the stage for the situation which calls forth the advice and to correct mistaken impressions."[3] This is precisely the way the *narratio* functions both here and in 1 Corinthians 1:11–17. Paul must correct the false impression that his gospel ministry had been stifled because he was under house arrest and perhaps also the impression that his situation was extremely desperate. It is clear enough that Paul is thankful for the support the Philippians have sent, but equally clear that he believes he could have done without it, perhaps in part because he anticipates his imminent release (compare 4:11–13 to 1:24–25). Furthermore, in order for the essential proposition (*propositio*) of this discourse to have real punch, Paul needed to provide his audience with at least one preliminary example of behavior to be followed and/or shunned, so that in 1:27, when he calls for a life worthy of the gospel, they will already have a clear idea of what he has in mind. In this manner, the *narratio,* by recounting a set of present facts about Paul's situation, sets the stage for the *propositio* in 1:27–30 and acts as part of the means of persuasion, though indirectly.

Paul is not merely reciting a few facts for general information; he is already engaging in persuasion by exciting positive feelings, such as empathy, for his situation. Quintilian stresses, "But what really carries greatest weight in deliberative speeches is the authority of the speaker. For he, who would have all men trust his judgment as to what is expedient and honorable [cf. Phil. 1:27], should possess and be regarded as possessing genuine wisdom and excellence of character" (*Inst. Or.* 3.8.12–13). Thus in this material we have a moving and emotional recounting of Paul's situation and more importantly a demonstration of how he showed and was showing grace under pressure, thus providing a positive example. He presents himself as one who exhibits the true behavior that leads to concord and unity, for he does not even allow rivalry or rivals to divert him from being thankful for the ongoing proclamation of the true gospel with good results.

In regard to rhetorical devices used in this subsection of the discourse we may point to the *inclusio* in vv. 12 and 25, where the theme of advancement or progress occurs at the beginning and end of the section.[4] There is also a careful and concise use of antithesis in vv. 15–17, again pointing to the care in the composition of this section.[5]

Translation

1:12 But I wish you to know, brothers [and sisters], that the things happening to me have led more to the progress of the gospel, **13**so that my chains in Christ have become evident among the whole of the Praetorian guard and all the others, **14**and the majority of the brothers [and sisters] [here] my chains have made [them] confident in the Lord, more than ever fearlessly daring to speak the Word.

15Some even through envy and rivalry, but others through goodwill preach Christ. **16**Those doing it out of love [do so] knowing that I am put here for the defense of the gospel, **17**but those others out of self-seeking proclaim Christ without pure motives, thinking to bring trouble to my chains. **18**For what [does it matter] save that in one way or another, whether due to pretext or truth, Christ is proclaimed, and in this I rejoice? **19**But also I will rejoice for I know that this will produce for me salvation through your petitions and the provision of the Spirit of Jesus Christ, **20**according to the eager expectation and my hope that in nothing will I be put to shame, but in all openness as always even now Christ will be glorified in my body, whether through life or through death. **21**For to me living [is] Christ and dying [is] gain. **22**But if living in the flesh, this means the fruit of work for me, and which I should choose, I do not know. **23**But I am caught between the two, having the desire to depart and to be with Christ, for that is much better. **24**But to remain in the flesh is more necessary for you. **25**And being confident of this, I know that I will remain and stay with all of you for the sake of your progress and joy of faith, **26**in order that your boasting in Christ Jesus in me may know no limits because of my coming back again to you.

Verse 12 begins a new section, and many have seen it as the beginning of the main body of the letter. In point of fact Paul's first full argument does not come until the second chapter, where Christ is presented as the paramount example for Christians in Philippi to follow. Yet the narration of facts and Paul's evaluation of how things will likely turn out serves the larger purposes of this deliberative letter. Paul will discourse for a while on his own circumstances but will apply an ethical lesson beginning in the *propositio* in vv. 27ff. The point of discoursing on his own example is parenetic; he is holding himself up as an example. Paul is explaining that, contrary to what one might expect, his being in chains has led to new opportunities to share the gospel with audiences he might not otherwise have reached. Far from being put out of commission, he has been placed by God in a strategic place so that he can witness to those close to the emperor, the Praetorian guard. As Lightfoot showed, the most common reference of the term *praetorium* in contexts like the present one is to a group of persons, not a place (see Tacitus *Hist.* 2.11, 1.20; Suetonius *Nero* 9).[6] There is no evidence of "Praetorium" being used for the headquarters of a proconsul in a senatorial province, for example, in Asia; thus, this term must count against an Ephesian imprisonment.[7] In fact, the word about Paul's witness has gotten out even beyond the Praetorian guard about Paul's witness. Paul does not say he converted all these people, but only that the witness has gone out, and so he has not ceased his life task while under house arrest.

Verse 14 also indicates that Paul's brave witness has encouraged many Christians who know about it (which surely means many where he is in Rome) to likewise bear fearless witness to God's word. These are in the majority (*pleionas*, v. 14). A minority, however, have taken Paul's imprisonment as an opportunity, apparently to try to make themselves prominent by displacing Paul in the eyes of other Christians. They proclaim the gospel for self-seeking reasons and impure motives. Paul does not say that these rivals are not proclaiming the real gospel, nor does he call them non-Christians. Thus, this group, living in Rome or nearby where Paul might readily hear about their activities, is not to be identified with the Judaizers who could afflict the Philippians and whom Paul will later warn about.[8] Nevertheless, Paul is able to warn his audience about the reality of rival teachers and preachers, and in this sense this material foreshadows and prepares for that in 3:1ff.[9]

Paul says, however, that whatever their motives, at least the gospel is being proclaimed, and for that Paul is grateful. This suggests that the proclamation of the true Word does not require a perfect messenger; God can write straight with crooked lines. Indeed one may ask if there is any other sort of humans, since all have sinned and fallen short of God's glory (Rom. 3:23). Paul believes that what converts is the Word of God, not the messenger. This should serve as a real antidote to an overinflated pastoral ego, both then and now. God can convert without us and even with those who preach out of envy, rivalry, or pretext or with impure motives.

It is difficult to know to what the *touto* ("this") in v. 19 refers. What is it that will result in Paul's salvation through the prayers of the Philippians and the work of the Spirit? Paul is here quoting exactly from Job 13:16 LXX, and the context of Job 13:13–18 is important there. The issue is Job's standing before God and his vindication.[10] This allusion likely tells us something about Paul's frame of mind, that by and large he expects vindication and release. Presumably, then, "this" refers to all the things that have happened to Paul, both good and bad, and he is reflecting on his own experience in light of that of Job. God will work these things out for Paul's ultimate good, and if things go badly, humanly speaking, God can provide a bountiful supply of the Spirit's aid so that Paul can endure and remain a good witness to the end.

Sōtēria (salvation) surely does not mean personal safety here, for v. 20 suggests that Paul will obtain *sōtēria* whether or not his trial turns out favorably. Furthermore, *sōtēria* elsewhere in Philippians also carries soteriological overtones (see 1:28, 2:12). Another interesting feature of this section is that Paul believes that his perseverance in the faith is in part dependent not only on the provision of the Spirit but also on the prayers of the Philippians.[11]

Paul knows a great deal about human frailty so he stresses that it is his eager desire and hope not to dishonor his Lord in whatever follows, whether life or death. He wants Christ glorified in his body, mind, and heart. In other words, he does not want his physical frailty to cause him to shrink back from the good witness. Hawthorne is probably correct that in v. 21 Paul means that for him living means Christ. This being so, to die is also gain because he will draw even closer to Christ.[12] It is right to stress that Paul does believe in a so-called intermediate state and sees death as an improvement on this life in terms of intimacy with Christ. As he says elsewhere, when Christians are absent from the body, they are present with the Lord (2 Cor. 5:6–7). This is why he can call dying gain.[13] But belief in life in heaven does not cause Paul to abandon his firm belief that the ultimate destiny for Christians is to be raised and made like Christ even in their bodies.

Verses 21–22 suggest that Paul's life, humanly speaking, may well now be hanging in the balance, but what he goes on to say suggests that he is confident that God is going to deliver him from his captors, for he still has work to do on behalf of the Philippians and others. Verse 23 depicts Paul as caught between two strong desires: the desire to go and be with Christ and the desire to stay and engage in more fruitful ministry. As Craddock remarks, it must seem more than a little strange to us to hear a prisoner talk about making a decision as to whether it is better to be released or be executed![14] Nevertheless, this reflects not only Paul's belief that God is in control of the situation, but also that mentally and spiritually Paul is on top of the situation. He will not be a passive victim whatever transpires. Thus in v. 25 Paul indicates his confidence that he will stay, since that is more necessary at this point in time. Paul did not suffer from an inferiority complex, but at the same time he knew that it was God who was working through him. Verse 26 depicts a scene in which Paul returns to Philippi and the Philippians are given something else to brag about, i.e., what God accomplished for and through Paul by delivering him from chains.

The language of boasting and honor in this passage reminds us that the Greco-Roman world had one set of values as to what amounted to honorable and shameful behavior and the Christian communities had another, though clearly there was some overlap. In a Roman setting like Philippi, honor was bound up with the public order, the doing of public works, and the behavior that bolstered the values of society and brought society's acclaim. Paul is trying in part in this discourse to de-enculturate his audience from such values by indicating that they are part of a different commonwealth, holding a different sort of citizenship; he thus uses different examples of what amounts to honorable or shameful behavior. The model for their behavior is not Caesar, with his displays of military power and public games, but Christ, who takes on the form of a slave (see Phil. 2). It needs to be understood that humility and servant-like behavior were not generally seen in the Greco-Roman world as admirable or even honorable, but rather in many cases were viewed as despicable and improper for a free person, especially a Roman citizen.[15] For Paul, however, the pattern of Christ's life, as encapsulated in the Christ hymn in Philippians 2, was also the pattern for ministry and for Christian life in general, i.e., self-chosen servanthood, followed by exaltation.

Apparently, "it is within the area of 'lifestyle' that Paul wants to establish the distinctive characterizations of a specific Christian identity."[16] Paul wishes to remap the zone of what amounted to honorable and what amounted to shameful or taboo behavior. It seems clear enough from this *narratio* that for Paul behavior that manifests loyalty to Christ and his model is considered honorable, while disavowing Christ and failing to try to model one's behavior on his example is considered shameful.

Paul, like others in his world, speaks of the public honoring of those who have upheld certain values and manifested certain public deeds, only for him it is God, not the local government or the citizens of Philippi, who is seen as the one who will ultimately do the honoring and whose standards one must live up to. The public acclaim for Christian works well done will come when Christ returns and one's deeds are finally evaluated and either rewarded or punished (see 1 Cor. 3). What is seen as honorable is behavior that benefits and builds up the Christian community and honors God in Christ. As I have said elsewhere,

> Paul is not in the business of simply baptizing the values of the larger cultural values of Roman society. To the contrary, he undermines many of their most cherished values and redefines what real status amounts to, namely, being in Christ and being sons and daughters of God. In Paul's book it is God, not society, who can bestow real honor and dis-

pense lasting shame. It is God, not society, including God in Christ, that is at the apex of Paul's pyramid of values, and as such only God is immune to Paul's telling criticisms of his world. Paul was attempting to set up a *counter*-culture with a set of values often at odds with the larger society.[17]

It is also true, nonetheless, that there were some values upheld by Paul in this letter that overlap those of the larger culture, for example, loyalty and faithfulness to one's friends or a concern for fairness and justice in human dealings. If one must put the accent in one place rather than another, however, Paul's counsel in this letter stresses the differences between the life pattern of a citizen of the heavenly commonwealth and that of a citizen of Rome. The emphasis on Paul as a source for the Philippians' boasting and pride is similar to what we find in 2 Corinthians 1:14.

There is a sense in which vv. 12–26 may be looked on as a typical missionary report, sent back to some of the missionary's financial supporters, allaying fears and rekindling hopes.[18] Paul had experienced severe adversity, but in fact these very adverse circumstances had provided new opportunities for ministry to those who might otherwise never have heard the gospel. The placement of this report of facts here makes good sense if Paul is following the normal placement of a *narratio* in a rhetorical discourse.

Chapter Five

The *Propositio* — 1:27–30

SOLID CITIZENS ON FIRM FOOTING

The essential function of a deliberative discourse is to persuade the audience to take some course of action in the present and/or future that will be honorable and, in the long run, to their advantage. The *propositio* amounts to the thesis statement explaining briefly what advice the orator urges on his audience.[1] He will state in a summary the basic course of action he wants his converts to take. The advice to be given in this letter then amounts to the following: the Philippians are to live in a way that is worthy of their Christian profession, which entails standing firm and together in one mind and spirit and not being led into schism or divisions by adversaries or even local church leaders offering bad teaching or bad advice. The various examples marshalled in this discourse, including the example of Christ, are meant to serve the end of promoting this essential advice offered in 1:27–30.

Quintilian makes two telling remarks about deliberative discourses that suit Philippians perfectly. First, all deliberative speeches are based simply on comparison (*Inst. Or.* 3.8.34). In Philippians Paul will persuade by means of comparing and contrasting various examples. Second, in all discourses the proposition should be lucid and preferably brief (*Inst. Or.* 4.5.26) as is certainly the case with Philippians 1:27–30.

Translation

1:27 Only live as citizens worthy of the Good News about Christ, in order that whether coming and seeing you, or being away, I may hear things concerning you that you stand firm in one spirit, one mind struggling together for the faith of the gospel. **28**And do not be afraid in anything concerning the adversaries, being proof of destruction to them, but salvation for you, and this from God, **29**that you be granted on behalf of Christ not only that you might believe in him, but also that you might suffer for him, **30**sharing the same contest such as you see in me and now you hear about me.

There are no major textual problems in this chapter.

Verse 27 is important, for it introduces the term *politeuesthe,* which means literally "to live as a (good) citizen." The social nuances of this term have often been glossed over in the standard commentaries, but it is hard to doubt that the Philippians would have picked up the implications. Paul's normal term when he wishes to talk about living a certain way is "walk" (*peripateō;* see Gal. 5:16). It is thus likely that Paul wishes to convey something more than just "live." *Politeuesthe* will come up in its cognate form when Paul in 3:20 speaks of the Philippians being citizens of a different sort of commonwealth, and this too points to the conclusion that Paul is appealing to the Philippians' sense of citizenship. This is of special relevance since Philippi was a Roman colony, inhabited by many Roman citizens.[2] Furthermore, many in the provinces were proud of their Roman citizenship, and probably some of the Philippian converts were among them.

As the comparison with 3:20 demonstrates, however, Paul is not simply encouraging the Philippians to be good citizens here or to do their civic duty, but rather to do their Christian duty.[3] Paul is going to make clear in 3:20 that he is calling the Philippians to be good citizens of a greater commonwealth than the Roman one and that being citizens of that commonwealth has very practical implications for how one will live in the here and now. One will take one's cues for living from the story and model of Jesus and of other faithful Christians like Paul, and not from the model of Caesar or other lords who were set forth as paragons of civic virtue in the larger society.[4]

Paul is in many respects using these citizenship terms much as Philo does in *De confusione linguarum* 77-78: "All whom Moses calls wise are represented as sojourners.... To them the heavenly region, where their citizenship lies [*en ho politeuontai*] is their native land; the earthly region in which they became sojourners is a foreign country." Paul's usage is somewhat less ethereal than Philo's. He does not see heaven as inherently the believer's native land or final and eternal destination, but rather as the place where Christ now is and therefore the believer's temporary home after death and prior to the parousia (see 2 Cor. 5:1-10). Furthermore, Paul believes that in the person of Christ, heaven and the heavenly story about Christ have already invaded the earthly sphere, transforming that sphere and relativizing its institutions. In Paul's view, the *schēma* of this world is passing away (1 Cor. 7:31), and so one's allegiances must be primarily to those realities that are of enduring value and quality — the kingdom of God and the people of God. What needs to be understood about Paul's vision is that this is ultimately a world-transforming, not a world-negating vision; it is only the *present* form of this world that is passing away. Paul believed that when Christ returns to earth the kingdom, including resurrected believers, will be found here on earth, not in some ethereal realm beyond the material world.[5] Paul believes in an eschatological new creation and not just in spiritually renewed creatures. Thus, in the end, Paul differs from Philo in his vision of the believers' ultimate destiny and destination.

Paul's great concern is that the Philippians manifest the same consistent Christian character whether he is present with them or absent from them, and he realizes that this will not happen without struggle. The Philippians are to stand firm, being of one spirit and one *psuchē*. By these terms, Paul is not speaking of the parts of an individual Christian, but is stressing what the Philippians must share, one spirit and one *psuchē*. The latter Greek term could refer to their being of one mind or it could refer to their sharing in a common life.[6] The Philippians must stand together and struggle together in the faith lest they fall separately (i.e., as individuals). The Christian is not required to stand alone against the world but as part of the community of faith, bolstering, reinforcing, and strengthening one another. Paul views morality as a community event, something believers strive for together. They are called to stand as the body of Christ, not as severed members of it. Notice also that Paul sees suffering for the cause of Christ as an honor, something one should view as positive despite its painful character. The Philippians must stand firm and be ready.

The last clause of v. 27 is grammatically difficult and has prompted various conjectures including the odd translation of Lightfoot: "striving in concert with the faith."[7] I suggest that Silva is correct that in view of the context what is *meant* here is "contend together for the rule of life" (called "the faith") that characterizes the gospel.[8] The issue here is orthopraxy, a way of living, rather than orthodoxy. This conclusion is important, for it has bearing on the reference to the Philippians' adversaries in 1:28a. It is likely they were manifesting, in Paul's mind, an aberrant way of living out the gospel.

Thus, the reference in v. 28 to the adversaries, following hard on the heels of a discussion of the proper way to live as a Christian, is likely to be an allusion to the Judaizers who are criticized in chapter 3, which in turn provides another reason for not seeing 3:1ff., as part of some separate letter. That they are mentioned in the *propositio* suggests that Paul felt them important enough to be considered part of the essential subject matter of this discourse. In addition, if one allows a connection between 1:28a and 3:1ff. this likely moves the discussion in chapter 3 from the realm of the hypothetical to that of a critique of some actual current opponents of Paul and at least potentially of the Philippians.

Verse 28b is very difficult. The suggestion of Hawthorne that both clauses refer to the believers (the first clause from the opponent's viewpoint) is not credible.[9] The unity of the church in following a Christ-like lifestyle is a sign or proof of the adversaries' destruction, but points to the believers' salvation.

Verse 29 makes this interpretation more likely, for here Paul speaks of the real prospect of suffering for Christ, as Paul had.[10]

In v. 30 Paul uses the metaphor of a contest. He says to the Philippians, "You may have been spectators watching me contend for the faith but you may soon or already have entered the arena for the testing of your faith as well." Some of the most common metaphors for the Christian life Paul uses are athletic ones, in part because he wants to stress that being a Christian requires strenuous effort and ongoing discipline and often involves adversaries and pain. Rhetorically speaking this was an apt move in arenas like Philippi and Corinth (see 1 Cor. 9:24–27), where Greco-Roman games were considered important places for manifestations of public virtue and Roman character. In fact, Paul draws on the images of the games more in Philippians than in all his other letters.

As V. C. Pfitzner shows, we can find traces of such images in Philippians 1:27–30, 2:16, and especially 3:12–14.[11] Again here in the *propositio* a theme developed later in the letter is foreshadowed. Unlike in 1 Corinthians 9, the issue is not primarily the apostolic struggle or contest in and of itself, but the general Christian one, and thus in Philippians 3 Paul's struggle is seen as an example of the general Christian one, providing an example for the Philippians.

In closing the discussion of the crucial *propositio* it is well to ask in what sense is "the gospel...the charter of the Christian commonwealth" and in what way is Paul "asking them to live up to its claims"?[12] I would suggest that the gospel is the charter in that the narrative of Christ's life provides the pattern for Christian living.[13] Paul exhorts the Philippians to live up to its claims because he believes Christ-likeness not only is required, but also is ultimately the believer's destiny. God is working in their midst (and they must work out what God works in) to produce such likeness spiritually and ethically in the present (as one dies to sin and lives to God) and physically at the resurrection. Even the so-called doctrinal sections of this letter, including both the Christ hymn in chapter 2 and the various references to resurrection throughout, in fact serve largely parenetic purposes, showing the Philippians both the pattern and the goal of the Christian life. Christ's history is viewed as the believer's destiny, *and* as J. H. Schütz puts it, "the gospel establishes the norm of the Philippians' conduct."[14] We must now see how this is worked out in the first major argument of this letter, which begins at 2:1ff.

Chapter Six

The *Probatio* — 2:1–4:3

THE FIRST APPEAL:
THE EXAMPLE OF CHRIST — 2:1–18

We have now arrived at the argument, or *logos*, section of this letter, and it is no accident that here, especially in vv. 1–11, we find some of Paul's most lyrical and rhetorically effective prose, indeed vv. 6–11 may even be said to be poetic in character.[1] Keep in mind that in a deliberative speech the aim of the arguments, "proofs," or appeals is to provide reasons for the hearer to take up the course of action being advised. Some of the most effective appeals in a deliberative argument are those not only to historical examples but also to the experience of the audience, and it is clear that at the beginning of this first argument Paul uses the Philippians' Christian experience as a basis for the plea for unity that follows. In general, arguments that depend on an appeal to *pathos* are more dependent on style and tone of delivery than arguments that appeal to logic. This may partially explain why we have some of Paul's most rhetorically adept prose in 2:1–4. "Since Paul uses such emotive arguments even in his letters, I suspect he chose his messengers to deliver and *perform* these letters with some consideration of their speaking abilities so that these nuances would not be missed by the audience."[2] One must bear in mind that in a Roman colony and in a congregation made up largely of Gentiles, rhetorical performance would be an important factor in giving credence to someone's words.

In a deliberative argument for concord and unity there are two normal sources of disunity that the rhetor must deal with: opponents from without who are troubling the audience, and factionalism from within. In chapter 2 Paul is dealing with the internal factors that lead to unity, and behavior (such as that mentioned in 2:3a, 14–16) that can destroy unity. A specific example of factionalism or internal squabbles in the Philippian congregation will be dealt with in the closing argument of the *probatio* in 4:2–3. That passage has led D. E. Garland to propose that all the preceding argument has been leading up to Paul's brief attempt to resolve this problem in the local Philippian leadership.[3]

F. Stagg puts it this way:

> How could Euodia and Syntyche continue their quarrel in the presence of him [Christ] who surrendered his rights and privileges for the sake of others...? How can they persist in their divisive quarreling in the presence of their own [Epaphroditus] who gambled his very life in devotion to both Paul and his own church?[4]

For that matter how could they act this way in the presence of Timothy, who acts self-sacrificially, or in light of the example set by Paul?[5] There is merit to this line of thinking, as Paul often reserves more difficult matters until the close of a discourse, hoping that the rhetoric that has gone before prepares the way for dealing with the most difficult problem (e.g., 2 Corinthians). It is too much to suggest, however, that the function of all that precedes 4:2–3 simply prepares for that appeal. Paul has a variety of concerns in this letter, including tactfully thanking the Philippians for Epaphroditus and the gift he brought (this matter probably is separate from that discussed in 4:2–3). What unifies this letter is the appeal to unity and the arguments against a variety of problems both internal and external that threaten to undo that unity.

While it is likely a correct observation that the severity of the problem of factionalism in Philippians pales in comparison to that in Corinth, it is wrong to overlook the pointers in Philippians that there are significant factors pulling the congregation in various directions. The sixteen references to joy in this letter should not cause us to overlook the equally earnest appeals for unity. Paul rejoices over the good things happening in the

Christian life of the Philippians, but there are factors that must be dealt with if Paul's joy is to be complete or full.

Since at least the time of Aristotle there was general agreement that "examples [*paradeigmata*] are most suitable for deliberative speakers, for it is by examination of the past that we divine and judge the future" (Aristotle *Rhetoric* 1.9.40; see also Cicero *De Or.* 2.335). Quintilian stresses that "examples are of the greatest value in deliberative speeches, because reference to historical parallels is the quickest method of securing assent." He adds, "It matters a great deal whose authority is adduced and to whom it is commended" (*Inst. Or.* 3.8.36). The function of such examples is to provide a solid basis for the appeal to imitation. What we see in Philippians 2 is Paul wisely putting his best foot forward and appealing first to the ultimate example of behavior that produces concord and unity: the example of Christ. Christ by his actions created a new community manifesting *koinōnia*. The Philippians are to have the same disposition among them as existed in Christ and was demonstrated by his behavior. Paul must show that it is to the advantage or benefit of the Philippians if they emulate such *exemplars* as Christ, Paul, Timothy and others.[6]

Perhaps because of the enormous attention the Christ hymn in 2:6–11 has attracted, insufficient attention has been paid to how 2:1–4 prepares the way for presentation of the first example in 2:6–11. The key link is to be seen in the reference to "mind" (twice in 2:2 and again in 2:5). One must ask how the hymn functions especially in light of 2:5, and the answer must be that it provides the ultimate example of the sort of disposition Paul is inculcating in his converts in 2:1–4. The story of Christ is the paradigm and pattern for the life of the believer in a variety of ways, though there are also a variety of ways in which Christ was unique and his experience not imitable.[7]

Translation

2:1If then [there is] any appeal in [the example of] Christ, if any persuasive power of [God's] love, if any sharing together of the Spirit, if any affection and compassion, 2complete my joy in order that you may think the same thing, having the same love, sharing a common life, being concerned for the one [unity], ³not according to personal advantage/party spirit nor according to empty glory but in humility thinking of one another better than of one's own self, ⁴each looking out not for one's own interests, but [also] everyone* [looking out for] the others [interests]. ⁵Have this frame of mind among you which also [was] in Christ Jesus, ⁶who

PART I Being in the form of God,
Did not consider the being equal to God
Something to take advantage of,
⁷But stripped/emptied himself
Taking the form of a servant
Being born in the likeness of human beings†
⁸And being found in appearance like a human being,
Humbled himself, being obedient to the point of death,
even death on the cross.

PART II ⁹That is why God has highly exalted him
and has given him the Name, the one above all names
¹⁰in order that at the name of Jesus
all knees will bend—heavenly, on earth, and under the
    earth
¹¹and all tongues confess publicly that
Jesus Christ is LORD
unto the glory of God the Father.

¹²So then my beloved, just as you always obey, not only as when I return, but also now much more in my absence, with fear and trembling do your best to bring about your own [common] salvation. ¹³For God is the one active/energizing among you both to will and to act according to his good pleasure. ¹⁴Do all this without grumbling and argument ¹⁵in order to become blameless and guileless children of God, unblemished in the midst of a crooked and perverse generation in which

---

*In 2:4 the plural *hekastoi* is to be preferred as the more difficult reading.
†In 2:7 the plural of *anthrōpos* is to be preferred, the singular being an attempt at conformity to the singular *doulos*.

you shine as luminaries in the cosmos, [16]holding fast the living word for my boasting at the day of Christ, that I may not run in vain nor engage in empty labor, [17]but if also I pour myself out upon your sacrifice, even a religious service [that springs from] your faith, I rejoice and rejoice with all of you, [18]but in the same way also you [must] rejoice and rejoice with me.

There are no major textual problems, but numerous grammatical ellipses.

Philippians 2:1–4 has been very carefully composed, manifesting a clear three-part structure, as has been demonstrated by D. A. Black.[8] First, there are four "if" clauses speaking of the ground of unity in 2:1, followed by a chiastic structure in v. 2, where the first and last clauses focus on the same subject from two slightly differing angles (being of one mind or disposition and having the same aim or goal) as do the middle two (maintaining the same love, which is to say sharing a harmonious common life).[9] This verse focuses on the attitude or disposition in the community that can produce unity. This in turn is followed in vv. 3–4 by an A, B, A, B, structure contrasting what the Philippians are and are not to do: selfishness is contrasted to self-humbling behavior; concern for self-interests is contrasted with concern for the interests of others. This verse stresses the outward behavior that is the appropriate manifestation of a disposition inclined toward harmony and unity. Verse 5 then is to be seen as the key link between this exhortation and the example that follows in 2:6–11, which provides the most compelling argument for such attitudes and behavior. The hymn is followed by a further exhortation in vv. 12–18 based upon what has come before in both 2:1–5 and 6–11. Verses 1–18 then as a whole must be seen as an exhortation to unity that involves inculcating the proper attitude and humble mutual service, with the example of Christ appealed to as a model. The parenetic function of the Christ hymn should be clear from its introduction. The intent here is to build up the body of Christ in Philippi.

The importance of this initial argument should not be underestimated. As Bloomquist shows in some detail, its vocabulary and ideas recur throughout the whole letter,[10] showing that this is the central and primary argument of the discourse and that the behavior cited here is the pattern to be played out in the other positive examples, including Paul's own example to his converts.[11]

The chapter begins with a series of incomplete phrases each beginning with *ei* (if). The function of these phrases is not to cast doubt on the fact that there is indeed some encouragement or appeal in Christ's example, for these are not real conditional protases in the usual sense. One can say the condition is already an actual one.[12] It should also be noted how closely this chapter is linked by *oun* to the *propositio* that immediately precedes it in chapter 1. This transitional particle could be translated "then," but it is even possible to translate it "first." In short, Philippians 2 builds on the truths expressed in 1:27-30 and reiterates some of them more fully.

Chapter 2 already hints that whatever problems there are in Philippi, they are caused by disunity and dissension, which Paul proposes to remedy by: (1) exhortation; (2) sending two of his cohorts; and (3) finally coming himself if possible. Throughout this section it is crucial to bear in mind that Paul is addressing the Philippians as a group, an *ekklēsia*. For example, when he says, "if there is any *koinōnia* of the Spirit," he means, if there is any sharing in common or participation in the Spirit by the group collectively, not if various individuals share on their own in the Spirit. The Philippians do have the Spirit in common and thus there is all the more reason why they should express their unity in the Spirit.[13]

This last clause tips us off to the drift of the first three "if" clauses, as Lohmeyer saw clearly.[14] As he notes, the third "if" clause has exactly the same phrase as in the benediction in 2 Corinthians 13:13: the *koinōnia pneumatos*. This in turn leads one to think that the first clause has to do with what believers derive from Christ; the second with what one has from the Father; and the last with what one has from the Spirit. I have thus suggested in the translation that Paul is speaking of the appeal or ethical exhortation that the example of Christ provides, the persuasive power of God's love that they have, and the motivation that comes from their sharing in common in the Holy Spirit. It is the experience of God's work in their midst that is the ultimate motivator appealed to in 2:1–4 as is also the case in 2:12: they must work out the implications and manifestations of what God is working in them. In the final "if" clause Paul adds to this the feelings of affection and compassion the Philippians have (presumably for Paul). This last clause reveals the degree to which this argument is based on an emotional appeal.

Several of the expressions in v. 2 call for further comment. Paul exhorts them to think the same and to be concerned for "the one." As W. Barclay argued, the real sense of *phronein* in v. 2 is not merely "think" but rather a person's "whole attitude and disposition of mind."[15] The point here is that Paul is trying to inculcate a disposition that inclines these converts always to speak and act in such a way that harmony and unity are promoted. They are all to be concerned about "the one" and the oneness of the Body there. The two middle phrases in v. 2 also exegete each other. *Sumpsuchoi* literally means "having one *psuchē*." In view of Paul's use of *psuchē* elsewhere, this surely refers to the sharing of the same life principle or sharing a common life.[16] Another facet of this idea is expressed in the phrase "having the same love."

Verse 3 is meant to be contrasted with v. 2, explaining what does not comport with sharing a common disposition, a common love and life, namely, acting according to *eritheian*. This latter term can mean something like "personal advantage," but, as Lightfoot rightly stressed, its basic sense in the midst of a plea for unity is factiousness or "party spirit."[17] As such, it is to be associated with terms like *eris* (rivalry; see 1 Cor. 1:11; 3:3) and *stasis* (discord).[18] The second phrase says that the Philippians are not to be motivated by the desire for empty glory. It is hard to doubt that Paul has in mind his rivals, whether in Rome or in Philippi, who do act according to selfish values and on the basis of party spirit, and do strive after empty glory (see 1:15 and 1:17 to 3:19). The rivals provide examples to avoid. It was critical in early Christianity to stress group cohesiveness in an environment where religious pluralism of a sort and many gods were endorsed by the Empire. What was most dangerous to a fledgling movement was divisions from within caused by people professing to be Christians and trusted by unsuspecting converts. To combat this Paul often had to draw rather clear social, ethical, and theological boundary lines for his converts, lest the community be absorbed by various of the larger and already preexisting religions of the day.[19]

The word *tapeinophrosunē* in v. 3 is an important one deserving of some discussion. It has been rightly stressed that humility was not seen as a virtue in Greco-Roman antiquity. This word means something like "base-minded," "shabby," "of no account," and in its adjectival form it was no compliment at all (it meant having the mentality of a slave). This is perhaps in part where the pagan idea of Christianity as a slave religion comes from. It is true, however, that in the OT we see humility and lowliness exalted, for instance in the Psalms (10:17–18; 25:18; 31:7; see also Prov. 3:34, 11:2, 15:33; Job 5:11). Humility is also seen as a virtue in the Qumran literature (1QS 2:24). In view of Paul's indebtedness to the Wisdom tradition in his presentation of the Christ hymn, this may also be the case here in his use of this term.[20] Paul's most striking contribution to this development is that he connects this idea with the founder of his faith. Indeed, he sees Christ as Exhibit A of what humility does and ought to mean. Jesus was one who took the form of a slave or a servant (in view of the allusions to the servant songs in this hymn).[21]

The use of the term "humility" by Paul likely had social implications.[22] Social status was very important in the Greco-Roman world and, outside Italy, nowhere more so than in the Roman colonies. If Paul's advice in vv. 3–4 was taken seriously it would mean that those of higher status would have to stop acting on the basis of social distinctions and customs and rather take Christ's actions as their model for acceptable and commendable behavior toward any and all, especially toward Christians. In other words, the social implications of the advice here cut across the distinctions usually made between those of greater and lesser status, including the distinctions between patricians and plebians, citizens and non-citizens, and the *honestiores,* or more honorable ones, and the so-called *humiliores,* or less-honored and honorable ones.[23]

Verse 4 could be read in one of two ways. Paul could be saying that each person should *not* be looking out for his or her own interests, but rather everyone should look out for the other's interest. Some manuscripts (D,* F, G, K) do not have the *kai* after *alla*. *Kai* with *alla* would mean "but also," which would suggest that it is acceptable to look after one's own interests as well. I am suspicious of this *kai*, because it looks like a mollifying addition, but it is well supported by important and early manuscripts (p46, Aleph A, B, C, and others). One must bear in mind, however, that Paul is about to provide the example of Christ, who did *not* consider his own interests, rights, or advantage but rather set them aside for the sake of others. I suspect that Paul, like Jesus in the Sermon on the Mount, is saying, Don't worry about your own interests but be concerned about others. He is calling Christians to be self-forgetful, as the following example of Christ suggests. Thus I leave the word "also" in brackets in the translation.

I agree with Hawthorne that v. 5 parallels the frame of mind believers ought to have, and the frame of mind Christ both as preexistent one and as incarnate one is said to have had in the hymn.[24] He deliberately took a lower place. He deliberately did not take advantage of the divine prerogatives that were rightfully his. He deliberately submitted to death on a cross, a punishment reserved for the most notable and notorious ne'er-do-wells of antiquity. It is worth adding that Paul is talking about a social attitude that affects behavior within the Christian community ("have this mind/disposition *among yourselves*"), not merely an internal disposition in individual Christians.[25] This requires, as is most common, that we assume that the omitted verb in the clause "which [mind] also _____ in Christ Jesus" is some form of the verb "to be."[26] The suggestion that Paul means something like "have this mind in you which you have in Christ," besides requiring redundancy, overlooks that we are dealing with an analogy and that 2:5 is bridging what has been said of and to the converts and what will be said about Christ as their example.[27] The oft-repeated arguments, based on the treatment of E. Käsemann,[28] are an overreaction to the idea of Christ as example and are well answered by F. Stagg: "The protest that one cannot imitate Christ by becoming incarnate, dying on the cross, and being exalted to heaven is caricature, not exegesis."[29] An analogy involves points of similarity in the midst of obvious differences; in this case a similar attitude and similarly self-sacrificial behavior are being commended to produce unity in the Philippian congregation.[30]

One must ask the question, What happens to social hierarchies in the Christian community when they come under the searchlight of an ethic that calls on everyone to serve and consider the interests of others? By this schema, leaders become at most exemplary or head servants, and Roman pecking orders become irrelevant or even obsolescent *within the life of the community.* In this regard the Christian community seems to have acted rather like some ancient clubs, trade guilds, and societies (*collegia*) in that a more egalitarian approach was taken and even slaves were allowed to have their say and assume some leadership roles.[31]

At this point we must comment in detail on the Christ hymn. The literature on this material in 2:6-11 is enormous and the discussion of it easily fills up whole monographs.[32] Since I have demonstrated elsewhere that this early hymn should be evaluated in light of other similar hymnic materials (see, e.g., Col. 1 and John 1) that manifest the common pattern of preexistence, earthly existence, and post-existence, and ultimately should be seen in light of the Hebrew Scriptures[33] and especially the Jewish Wisdom material, particularly in regard to the role of Christ in creation, I do not propose to rehearse all that here.[34] Rather I will confine myself to some comments about the content and function of this material as Paul shapes and uses it.

Three words are used to describe Christ that have overlapping fields of meaning — "form," likeness, or appearance (*morphē, homoiōmati, schēmati*). Of these three the one that most obviously connotes outward recognizable appearance is *schēmati. Schēmati* always suggests the way in which a thing or person appears to our senses.[35] However, *morphē* normally signifies an outward form that truly, accurately, and fully expresses the real being that underlies it. Thus when applied to Christ it must mean that he manifested a form that truly represents the nature and very being of God. This is why we have the further phrase "the being equal to God."[36] The hymn makes clear that Christ really has this. As for the third term, *homoiōmati,* it does mean likeness, but again the sense is not an illusory outer appearance that belies the real nature, but that Christ really took on human likeness.

The word *harpagmos* has caused endless debate and dispute. Traditionally it has been taken to mean either (1) robbery, in which case the verse reads that Christ did not consider it robbery to be equal to God (i.e., he was no usurper or interloper grabbing for more than what was rightfully his), or (2) that Christ did not consider being equal to God a matter of clutching on to his rightful divine prerogatives. This latter translation makes better sense of the text. An extensive and persuasive discussion by R. W. Hoover has shown that the real issue concerns the meaning of *harpagmos* when combined with the verb *hēgeomai.* This "idiomatic expression refers to something already present and at one's disposal," and thus one may translate the key phrase: Christ "did not regard being equal with God as . . . something to use for his own advantage."[37] This makes very good sense in light of 2:4: Christ becomes the ultimate example of one who did not pursue his own interests or selfishly take advantage of rights, privileges, or status that were properly his, but rather "emptied himself."

It is important that we give full weight to the contrast between vv. 6b and 7a: Christ did not see being equal with God something he had to take advantage of; rather, he stripped himself ("emptied himself"). Hawthorne is too anxious to deny that Christ stripped himself of anything when he became incarnate.[38] However, the verb "stripped" or "emptied" must have some content to it, and it is not adequate to say Christ did not subtract anything since in fact he added a human nature. The latter is true enough, but the text says that he did empty himself or strip himself. What it does not tell us explicitly is of what he emptied himself. The contrast between vv. 6b and 7a is very suggestive; that is, Christ set aside his rightful divine prerogatives or status. This does not mean he set aside his divine nature, but it does indicate some sort of self-limitation, some sort of setting aside of divine rights or privileges. To phrase the matter in traditional theological terms, it may mean that Paul thinks Christ did not draw on his ability to be omnipotent, omnipresent, and omniscient (i.e., he accepted human limitations of time, space, and knowledge). In Paul's view, he could have drawn on these abilities had he wanted to, but he resisted the temptation to push the "God-button." Rather, he lived among us as one of us who drew on the power of the Spirit, the guidance of the Word, and the use of prayer through which God revealed much to him.

Christ not only stripped himself in this way, but also shunned any rightful human accolades or glory. He pursued a course of status reversal, and as a result God returned the favor, exalting him to even greater heights than he had before he took on human form, if that were possible. As the text says, he took on the very form of a servant or slave, he identified himself with the lowest of the low, and he died a slave's death.

This hymn places a special stress on the fact that the preexistent Christ had a choice about these matters and he *chose* to act in the way he did. Thus, it is stressed that Christ was *obedient* even to the point of dying on the cross. He could have done otherwise. The reason for this stress is that Paul is engaging in *imitatio Christi.* Paul does not think it is ridiculous idealism to appeal to the example of Christ as a moral pattern for believers. Rather, he believes that by God's Spirit and grace believers too can be obedient even unto death.

Hawthorne goes on to point out in this hymn that Paul seems to stress the gospel principle that those who humble themselves (an action, not an inferiority complex) will be exalted (see Matt. 23:12). If this is so, then Paul is suggesting to his converts that there will be a crown of glory for them as there was for Christ, whom God exalted to the highest place.

The first half of the hymn refers to behavior by Christ that the believer is called upon to imitate, while the second half refers to God's response to such behavior. Paul does indeed believe that Christians are in the process of being and will finally be conformed to the image of Christ, even sharing a similar resurrection body. He believes further that there is reward for believers who do good works (see 1 Cor. 3) and are obedient, especially those who, like Christ, suffer for him and perhaps even die like him (see Phil. 3:10).[39] Paul is not speaking here of an automatic sequence of events but of a deliberate act on God's part.... In other words, to speak of a logical consequence does not exclude the question of whether or not a personal reward is in view.... The Christ-hymn implies a correspondence between Christ's experience and the believer's sanctification leading to glorification, not between Christ's exaltation and the sinner's justification. Surely believers are exhorted to persevere in their Christian race so they may receive the prize (Phil. 3:13–14), but we need not for that reason fear that the notion of reward conflicts with Paul's doctrine of justification (Rom. 4:5 ...).[40]

Just as Christ's act of obedience was vindicated by God, so too this will be the case in the life of the believer.[41] Believers "are called to see in Jesus' action not only the basis of their obedience but also its pattern and direction."[42] This does not imply full identification in end result, however, for the believer does not become Lord to whom all will bow.

The name that is above all names is the name of God, and in this hymn the name that Jesus is given when he is raised and exalted beyond death is not Jesus (he had that name since human birth) but rather the name of God in the OT, Lord, which is the Septuagint equivalent to Yahweh.[43] At the name of Jesus all will bow and recognize his new and rightful title, Lord, when history ends. It may be that this implies the unwilling recognition by opponents, or perhaps Paul has the eschatological scene in view that transpires after the final judgment when all negative forces and beings have been dealt with and are no longer on the scene. The former is more likely since vv. 10–11 suggests that all sentient beings (left) will make this confession, including angels, humans, and demons. This does not necessarily mean then that all will in the end be converted. It does mean all will be forced to recognize the truth, as the demons whom Jesus exorcised did in the gospel tradition, but their true confessions helped them not, for they were not transformed by that truth (see Mark 5:1–20).

The importance of the partial quotation of Isaiah 45:23 in Philippians 2:10–11 should not be underestimated, for this scriptural echo comes from a context where it is said that "I am the Lord [Yahweh], and there is none else...there is no other God besides me.... Turn to me and be saved all the ends of the earth.... I have sworn by myself...that to me every knee will bow, every tongue will swear allegiance" (45:18–25). Jesus then is praised using both the language and title deemed appropriate only for Yahweh in this Isaianic text.

Notice that confessing "Jesus is Lord" (the earliest Christian confession) does not detract from but in fact adds to the Father's glory, for God has made this all possible by raising and exalting Jesus. This is not because Paul believes Christ to be something less than divine in character, but because Jesus has become part of Paul's new Christian definition of what monotheism amounts to (see 1 Cor. 8:6).[44] Christ contributes to, rather than detracts from, what the Godhead is and does. He bears Yahweh's title to the glory of God.[45]

Of consequence for our study is I. H. Marshall's reminder that the verb *huperupsōsen*, which means "to raise exceedingly high," was used metaphorically of assigning a person to a high status so that that person received honor, obedience, praise, and submission from other people of lower status (see Ps. 97:9).[46] In terms of the function of this Christ hymn in the matrix of Paul's advice given in this first argument to his converts, two things are suggested by this language. First, living out the social implications of being a follower of Jesus includes acting in status-rejecting ways and even being prepared to suffer the extreme penalty, reserved for the likes of slaves. When one has as a model a servant leader who willingly takes on a much lower status and servile roles, one may expect not only to perform self-abasing acts, but also to experience public humiliation, suffering, and even death. Second, one must nevertheless evaluate such actions and outcomes not from a Greco-Roman perspective, but rather from God's perspective — as actions that deserve to be praised and vindicated at the eschaton. Christians are part of a commonwealth that has a very different set of codes about what amounts to honorable behavior, status, and reward.[47]

It is instructive to compare this passage to 2 Corinthians 8:9: "For you know the grace of our Lord Jesus Christ, that though he was rich, yet for your sakes he became poor, so that you through his poverty might become rich." Here too Paul uses the language of changing one's social status to refer to Christ's condescension, not only in taking on human form, but also in dying the death of the disenfranchised in order to exhort his converts to similarly generous and selfless actions. As Chrysostom puts it, "Nothing rouses a great and philosophic soul to the performance of good works so much as learning that in this it is likened to God. What encouragement is equal to this? None."[48]

Christ's career must cause a transvaluation of values even in regard to something as repulsive as death on the cross. The following comment of Cicero is typical and shows how far Paul is calling his converts from the standard evaluations of what amounted to honorable and dishonorable ends: "To bind a Roman citizen is an outrage; to scourge him a crime; it almost amounts to parricide to put him to death; how shall I describe crucifixion? No adequate word can be found to represent so execrable an enormity" (*Inv.* 5.66).[49] As Barclay remarked:

> Here then is the final appeal of Paul to the Philippians. If Jesus Christ was prepared to accept this amazing humiliation, how can His followers quarrel among themselves about matters of honour and of precedence? Surely all human thoughts of the exaltation of self must shrivel up before the memory of the amazing sacrificial selflessness of Jesus Christ.[50]

Moving on to vv. 12ff. we may note a return to the imperative mode of speaking found in 2:1–5. Watson suggests that we see this as a second development of the *propositio,* and there is no denying that this subsection deals with various themes mentioned in the announcement of themes in 1:27–30.[51] Because (1) the *hoste* (therefore) clearly links 2:12–18 with the Christ hymn,[52] making clear that Christ's example is the basis of the appeal that follows, and (2) these verses are based upon it and upon the earlier part of the argument in 2:1–5, I would prefer to see this section as the concluding portion of the first appeal or argument. This would mean that the first argument has an A (imperative), B (indicative), A (imperative) format. It is clear, however, that Paul is appealing to the Philippians' emotions, evoking *pathos* by alluding both to their situation and his own possible impending death on their behalf.[53] The first argument then manifests the three parts of an overall discourse: *ethos* (and some *pathos,* 2:1–5), *logos* (2:6–11), and *pathos* (2:12–18) in a masterful way. The emotional appeal in this last segment can be seen in the use of the phrase "my beloved," the reference to "fear and trembling," and the reference to being poured out as a libation on a sacrifice.

It would appear that v. 12 refers to Paul's coming or return to Philippi (*parousia* normally has the sense of coming, not merely presence). Paul seems to anticipate that this will happen. Since v. 12c is so often misused, we should look at it closely. Paul says that even in his absence the Philippians (you *plural*) should, with awe and reverence, do their best to bring about their *sōtēria.* This could mean well-being (i.e., shalom), or it could have a social sense of bringing about the harmony and well-being of the community.[54] Note that he is not exhorting each individual to pursue his or her own interest in this matter. Since he has just asked them to be self-forgetful, it is not likely he would have reversed himself here. The question then becomes, What collective, corporate, and common goal is he urging upon his converts?

While I would not rule out the social interpretation of this crucial verse, it seems more likely that here, as elsewhere when Paul uses the term *sōtēria* (including the uses in this very letter; see 1:28), he has eschatological reality in mind, not merely a social condition of the community.[55] This conclusion is certain if one allows a close connection between 1:28 and 2:12, the latter further developing the theme announced in the former verse. It follows from this that the exhortation does have a social dimension or implication. One must ask what it would mean to work out the shared common gift of eschatological salvation from God, which is also still in part a goal. In short, the appeal to unity is based on what God has already done and is doing in them and in their midst to bring about their salvation. Working out salvation means, among other things, continuous strenuous effort working harmoniously together as the body of Christ.

They are to work together with a sense of awe and even trem-

bling,[56] not only because God is in their midst energizing them
to will and do, but also because God will hold them accountable for their behavior and social relationships. That behavior
affects obtaining the goal (see 3:12–14). The phrase "fear and
trembling" is in an emphatic position in the Greek text, indicating that Paul is emphasizing this proper attitude. One must
always be mindful that God is watching and will hold the believer accountable for his or her actions.[57] Paul wishes to be
proud of them at the "day of Christ," a phrase that refers to the
day of judgment and occurs in this form only in Philippians (see
1:6, 10; 2:16). It may be that this is stressed in this letter because Paul is emphasizing that final and full salvation comes for
believers on the day of judgment when they are conformed to
Christ's image; hence the reference to Christ in association with
"that Day" is meant to put a positive cast on the concept (see
3:20). Believers eagerly await a Savior to return on that day.

Paul hastens to add in v. 13 that they *can* and should be doing
this, *for* God is active in energizing or arousing them both to
will and to do this very thing according to God's good pleasure.
They are to work out what God is enabling them to will and to
do toward bringing about a united loving body of Christ as the
locus of salvation.

Verse 14 likely alludes to the Israelites who grumbled in the
wilderness, especially since v. 15 involves a partial quote of Deu-
teronomy 32:5, which refers to these Israelites as a sinful and
deceitful generation. Paul says they must not be like that, but are
rather to be guileless and blameless, unblemished in the midst of
a crooked generation, like stars shining in a very dark sky. Here,
as in 1 Corinthians 10, Paul is using the negative example of the
behavior of the Israelites in the wilderness to tell his converts
how *not* to behave. This allusion may prepare for the discussion
in Philippians 3:1ff., where Paul mentions the enemies of the
cross. This conclusion is suggested by two factors. First, the allusion here is to the unfaithful and grumbling *among* God's people
who are contrasted with the Philippians when they act properly.
It might seem peculiar for Paul to contrast the Philippians with
a group of God's people, until we realize that it was likely Jewish
Christians, who claimed to be among the elect, who were ap-

parently giving the Philippians trouble. Second, while we might expect Paul to be alluding to Gentiles in the use of the phrase "crooked and perverse generation," Paul will go on in Philippians 3 to adopt the polemical term "dogs," usually used by Jews against Gentiles, to refer to the Judaizing Christians troubling the Philippians. The not so subtle implication in both contexts is that "not all Israel is of Israel," or in this case not all claiming to be Jewish Christians are part of God's people, and thus their advice and example should be shunned. This may be called reverse polemics, the adoption of epithets normally used against Gentiles by Jews to paint a dark portrait of Jewish Christian opponents. If the above conclusions are correct, then this provides a strong argument for seeing Philippians 3:1ff. as always a part of the same letter as Philippians 2:12-18.[58]

In order for the Philippians to be stars in a dark sky or shining examples in a wicked generation, they must hold fast to the living word Paul has proclaimed and written to them. It is possible to translate the verb *epexō* as "hold forth" rather than "hold fast" the word of life, in which case this becomes a missionary appeal about being the light of the world. Two things count against this conclusion, however. First, both the preceding and following discussions suggest that Paul is trying to sort out problems preventing unity in the Philippian congregation. This letter uses examples to appeal for unity, not for witnessing. Second, Philippians 3 quite clearly is about protection from, not witnessing to, opponents.

Verse 17 uses the striking metaphor of sacrifice. Paul considers it a real possibility, though perhaps not likely right away, that he may be poured out like a drink offering over the sacrifice of the Philippians. It seems that Paul has the procedure of a pagan sacrifice in view, since the majority of his audience were probably Gentiles.[59]

Of what does this sacrifice consist? Strongly in favor of the conclusion that *thusia* may refer to the sacrificial monetary offering the Philippians sent to Paul is the fact that Paul uses the imagery of sacrifice both here and in 4:18; in the latter text the reference is clearly to the monetary gift. Furthermore, Paul uses *leitourgias* not only in 2:30 to refer to the Philippians' gift, but also in 2 Corinthians 8:2 to refer to a monetary gift. This is likely to be the thrust of the word here, which we translated as "a religious [and public] service." The issue then in 2:17–18 is the same as that in 1:5: the Philippians' participation in Paul's ministry,[60] a ministry that may result in Paul's death for the cause. Paul is suggesting that the Philippians have made the greater sacrifice to which his death would only add the crowning touch.

> Paul's focus of attention is upon the sacrificial service . . . of the Philippians. Theirs is the main sacrifice offered to God. The apostle is willing that, if one thing remains to make that offering perfectly acceptable, his own life be sacrificed . . . and be credited to their account. But he describes that pouring out of his life in death by means of the modest *drink* offering.[61]

The proper conclusion to be drawn from this metaphor is that Paul believes his work will have been in vain if the Philippians do not successfully run the good race and finish the course; his libation is of no consequence if the sacrifice (not only embodied in the monetary gift, but much more so in their whole Christian lives) is not properly offered.[62] Yet the Philippians have been obedient in the past and Paul has good reason to think they will continue to be so. In a Greco-Roman sacrifice, if it was in any way improperly offered, it had to be done all over again.

Even if (and Paul does say "if" here[63]) Paul may be killed for their faith, the Philippians should rejoice in this, as Paul will count it a privilege to die for the faith, for Christ, for his people. Here Hawthorne's whole case for Caesarea as the location from which the letter was written is very weak, as is the case for those who argue for an Ephesian imprisonment.[64] This verse, if it is not to be seen as idle speculation, must place Paul in a location where he was in real danger of execution *by Roman authorities* — which must favor Rome. Otherwise, Paul still had another appeal to avoid the axe.

Chapter Seven

The *Probatio* — 2:1–4:3

THE SECOND APPEAL:
THE PARADIGMATIC PARTNERS — 2:19–30

Duane Watson argues that 2:19–30 should be seen as a digression within the *probatio,*[1] but I suggest that the function of this section is not primarily to praise or blame persons, make an emotional appeal, amplify topics, or enhance style, the basic functions that first-century teachers of rhetoric ascribe to a digression (see Cicero *Inv.* 1.51.97; Quintilian *Inst. Or.* 4.3.12–15). Rather, what we have here is the second development of the appeal for unity, only this time Timothy and Epaphroditus serve as the examples. A variety of scholars have rightly pointed to the close connection between the language of the Christ hymn and that of 2:19–30 (e.g., see *hēgesato* in 2:6–7 and 2:25; *mechri thanatou* in 2:8 and 2:30; Christ as *doulos* in 2:7 and Timothy *edouleusen* in 2:22).[2] Part of the rhetorical function of this material is to provide the audience with two examples of Christians who have followed Christ's example, but this is not all. Both Timothy and Epaphroditus through their sacrificial acts and attitude provide the examples of behavior that produces unity and concord. Paul will also stress how both of these leaders are his co-workers, fellow soldiers, having like goals and desires. Their relationship with Paul provides the social example of how things ought to be among and between the Philippians.

Scholars often treat the material in this brief section as yet another travelogue that assumes the formal structure of the apostolic *parousia* section of a letter.[3] In part because of this, it has sometimes been assumed that the letter must be near its

75

end. There are problems with both these assumptions. In the first place, there are various clear examples where Paul discusses his and/or his co-workers' travel plans well before the end of a letter (1 Cor. 4:17–19; 1 Thess. 2:17–3:6). This is no clear marker that the letter is drawing to a close. Second, of the five features that are said to make up the form known as the apostolic *parousia* section (a statement about the fact that the author is writing; a statement about the relationship between the author and audience; a discussion of a visit; an invocation of divine aid and approval of the visit; a mention of the visit's benefit), of the thirteen examples R. W. Funk cites from Paul only *one* item, namely, the third of these mentioned above, appears in all thirteen examples. In other words, these sections do not bear the consistent marks one would expect of a literary type, unlike, for instance, epistolary openings and closings of letters that have various elements regularly found in them. It would be much better to speak not of a travelogue *form* but rather, as T. Y. Mullin stresses, of the *theme* of travel, which takes on various forms and functions and appears as a major theme not only in Christian letters but also in the non-literary papyri.[4] Here it serves as part of Paul's second appeal to the Philippians for unity through sacrificial behavior and a Christ-like attitude, like that manifested by Timothy, Epaphroditus, and Paul.[5] Travel is not mentioned for its own sake or merely to indicate upcoming plans and movements, though that is part of the function, but to *affect the behavior of the audience,* guiding how they should respond when Epaphroditus comes with the letter, and later when Timothy comes, once he knows the outcome of Paul's trial. As such, it is part of the act of persuasion Paul is trying to perform in this discourse.

Translation

[2:19]But I hope in the Lord Jesus to send Timothy soon to you, in order that I also may be of good heart learning the things concerning you. [20]For I have no one else who is as alike in the depths of his being, such as genuinely cares about the things concerning you, [21]for all others are intent on their own affairs, not the affairs of Jesus Christ. [22]But you will know the proof of him, that as a father's child he served as a slave with me for the gospel. [23]This one then I hope to send as soon as ever I can look away from my own circumstances. [24]But I am persuaded in the Lord that even I also will come soon.

[25]But it is necessary to consider Epaphroditus the brother and my co-worker and fellow-soldier, but your "apostle" and delegated assistant of my need. [26]I am sending him to you since he is longing for all of you and much distressed because you heard that he fell ill. [27]For he was indeed sick near to death, but God had mercy on him, but not him only but also on me, in order that I might not have sorrow upon sorrow. [28]More eagerly then I send him in order that seeing him again you will also rejoice, being somewhat relieved. [29]Welcome him then in the Lord with all gladness, hold one such as this one in high honor, [30]because through the work of Christ he came near to death, risking life in order to fill up your lack of service to me.

In vv. 19–30 Paul speaks of two emissaries he is sending. Timothy, who earlier had the honor of being called a slave/servant (note the overlap in the OT and the Gospels between *diakonos* and *doulous*) of Christ, here is said to be like Paul's slave and child, serving him in a totally sacrificial manner. Paul says there is no one else as like in "soul" as Timothy is with Paul, and no one else who cares so much for the Philippians. The word *isopsuchos* is a rare one in Greek and not found elsewhere in the NT. One of the keys to understanding its meaning here is to bear in mind what Paul already said about the relationship between Christ and God the Father in 2:6: it describes a relationship of equality and similarity in character. In one respect this can also be said about the relationship of Paul and Timothy, namely, that they both share the same deep-seated love, concern, and "mind" for the Philippians. Perhaps an even more important parallel is found in Philippians 2:2, where the Philippians are urged to be one in common life (*sumpsuchoi*).[6] P. Christou argues that the term *isopsuchos* here has more of the sense of "confidant," but the second half of 2:20 suggests otherwise.[7] The point is that

Timothy is like-minded or shares the same feelings and heart attitude about the Philippians, and so we have offered an idiomatic rendering in the translation above. This may be because Timothy was involved with Paul in the conversion of the Philippians (see Acts 16:1ff., 17:14).

Verse 21 is of some importance since it likely alludes to those Christians in Rome, referred to in 1:15–17, who look out for their own interests. This tips us off that Paul once again is contrasting negative and positive examples for the Philippians to shun or follow, with a stress on two positive ones.[8] As soon as Paul can settle his own affairs (v. 23) he will send him. In v. 24, Paul again expresses the hope that he himself will come. It is instructive to see the language Paul uses about the three visits mentioned in this section: (1) Paul hopes to send Timothy; (2) he is confident he will come; and (3) it is necessary for him to send Epaphroditus back. The real surprise here is that Paul not only hopes to send Timothy but also is confident (in the Lord) that he himself will come!

The situation with Epaphroditus is a little different. The discussion here should be compared to the deliberative appeal in 1 Corinthians 16:15–17, not only because there are similarities in the appeal about a co-worker, but also because in both passages there is discussion about a messenger who fills up something lacking from the audience. In 1 Corinthians 16, Stephanas is being commended because Paul wants him to be recognized as a leader in Corinth who can help produce concord there.[9] Epaphroditus also is praised as a co-worker of Paul in the Lord, and one of the motives is so the Philippians will welcome and honor him when he returns. This would imply that Paul wants them to recognize that he completed his mission and to acknowledge his authority.[10] That he was the Philippians' gift-bearer and messenger to Paul also suggests his leadership role. Paul calls him "my fellow-soldier but your apostle."[11] The latter term may have its more generic sense of an envoy or messenger, a "sent one," but in view of the similar example in 2 Corinthians 8:23, where the envoys are involved in carrying money, it may be that Paul is using the term as the Greek equivalent to *shaliach*, an agent sent with a limited authority to carry out a specific task, often involving money or property.[12] In any case, the combination of the terms "co-worker," "fellow-soldier," and *apostolos* surely indicates that Epaphroditus was a leader in the Philippian congregation. This may be an unspoken reason why Paul finds it necessary to send him back.[13] The disunity in the congregation may have been caused in part by a power vacuum since Epaphroditus left.[14] He seems to have been a Gentile convert who became important in early Christian work in and for the Philippian church and is not to be confused with the Epaphras mentioned in Colossians 1:7, 4:12, or Philemon v. 23, who was from the Colossian church.[15]

A Closer Look: Between the Lines of 2:19-30

There are clues in this section about the provenance of this letter. We need to examine what Paul actually says about Epaphroditus. One must compare 2:17 to 2:25 and 30. In 2:25 the noun *leitourgos* appears and would seem to refer to the fact that the Philippians specifically commissioned Epaphroditus to deliver the money gift (note the use of *leitourgeō* in Rom. 15:27), for what is said is that he is the delegated assistant of Paul's need.[16] Now if Timothy is still with Paul, as this letter suggests, then surely what Paul means by his "need" is his financial need, something with which Timothy could not help Paul. In favor of this interpretation is Paul's reference to need when he is clearly discussing the Philippians' monetary gift in 4:11-12, and their earlier ministry to his financial need (*chreian*) while in Thessalonica in 4:16. Both 2:30 and 4:11-12 use the same language to refer to filling the lack of service that the rest of the Philippians could provide. This financial service was surely the main task Epaphroditus was assigned to do.

The importance of this has not escaped the notice of C. O. Buchanan, among others.[17] If it is said that Epaphroditus fell ill and risked his life in the course of carrying out the "service" he was commissioned to do, then this strongly suggests he fell ill while bringing the gift to Paul, *not* while he was with Paul. Elsewhere in his tribulation catalogs Paul makes very clear the sort of difficulties, dangers, and illnesses one could fall prey to while traveling the Roman roads (see 2 Cor. 11:23-27). Because of constant exposure to the elements, the danger of serious illness was considerably greater on the land journey from Philippi to Rome on the Egnatian Way than on board a ship from Philippi to Ephesus or to Caesarea Maritima. As G. B. Caird points out, if he fell ill prior to reaching Dyrrachium, then his family could have heard about it before he ever reached Rome.[18]

There is another consideration involved as well. If Paul had been under arrest in Ephesus and Epaphroditus had fallen ill on the way there, then it would have been a much shorter and easier matter for either Epaphroditus to return home quickly and find a substitute envoy, or for the Philippians to send help, or for Paul to write the Philippians quickly about the matter. As it is, the letter suggests a sufficient lapse of time between Epaphroditus's departure and Paul's writing of this document not only for the Philippians to have heard of Epaphroditus's illness, but also for Epaphroditus to have gotten well enough to be sent home. If Epaphroditus became ill and risked his life in the process of delivering the funds to Paul, having gotten too far from Philippi to turn back,[19] then we do not need to account for a much longer time between Paul's having received the gift and his reply thanking the Philippians.[20] Paul wrote back as soon as Epaphroditus was well enough to carry this Philippian letter back to the congregation in Philippi.

In other words, various hints and contingencies alluded to in Philippians 2:19–30 favor the view that Paul is writing from Rome and that the Philippians had heard about Epaphroditus's illness from some source other than Paul, probably from a Christian heading east who saw Epaphroditus somewhere along the Egnatian Way.[21] Finally, we have seen various hints in Philippians 1 and 2 that allude to the gift from Philippi and prepare for the fuller discussion of this delicate matter in 4:10–20. There is no good reason to take the key aorists and imperfects about sending in 2:19–30 as anything other than epistolary ones, as B. S. MacKay has shown,[22] and thus there is no need to separate 2:19–30 from 4:10–30 as if they were parts of two different letters.[23]

•

It seems most probable then that Epaphroditus fell ill and nearly died on the way to seeing Paul, but that he made it to Rome. Somehow the Philippians got wind of this, perhaps by a Christian whom Epaphroditus had met on the way who sent word back. In any case he recovered sufficiently to make the return journey of more than eight hundred miles. Paul is eager to send him back for four reasons. First, he is homesick. Second, the Philippians are anxious about him. Third, Paul will be relieved if the Philippians are relieved about Epaphroditus because he does not want them worrying unnecessarily. Fourth, Paul wants Epaphroditus to help sort out the dissensions in Philippi. This may be a delicate situation, because as a secondary purpose the Philippians may have sent Epaphroditus to be of some ongoing help to Paul. His coming back might be taken as a sign of failure or as a rebuff by Paul of a generous gesture. Thus Paul writes this letter in part to explain why Epaphroditus is coming back and should be honored, not shamed, for his return. It is partly written to smooth things over and to enable Epaphroditus to be of some ongoing ministerial use in Philippi as a respected leader.

There may be a charming word play in v. 30. The participle *paraboleusamenos*, which means "staked," "gambled," or "risked," may have been coined by Paul.[24] The name Epaphroditus means "favorite of Aphrodite," the goddess of gambling, whose name one would invoke for luck when rolling the dice. Thus Paul may be saying that Epaphroditus rolled the dice, but in the work of the Lord he staked his very life in order to fill up the lack of service the Philippians would not have been able to give otherwise. Paul is not saying that they owe him anything, but rather that they sent Epaphroditus because they felt a need to help, and he filled that need.

We may sum up the drift of the discussion in the two appeals in Philippians 2 as follows:

> First and foremost, Christ's example of lowly service (2:5–11) has been set forth as a powerful corrective to this attitude [of selfishness creating disunity]. Subsequently, Paul has referred to the possibility of his own life being poured out as a libation for others (2:17). He now presents Timothy, who has slaved selflessly in the gospel (2:22 see 1:1,7) and has a genuine concern for the interest of the Philippians (. . . 2:20), and Epaphroditus, who almost died in the *service* of Christ (2:30), as godly examples of the way the Philippians should imitate Christ. Thus 2:19-30 does not simply inform the Philippians about the apostle's plans for Timothy and Epaphroditus; the section also has a paraenetic purpose pointing to them as models of a selfless attitude that Paul wants the community to follow.[25]

A few concluding remarks are in order. One must be able to distinguish why Paul is sending Timothy and Epaphroditus to Philippi and why he writes about them as he does. This discourse is attempting to produce harmony and unity in the church in Philippi by setting forth examples, both positive and negative (as 3:1ff. more clearly shows), of self-sacrificial behavior that produces such harmony. Paul, however, is sending Epaphroditus back not only to further this aim, but also for the reasons stated in this passage. The function of the discourse and the function of the sendings overlap but are not identical.

Second, the language about knowing Timothy's proven worth or about honoring Epaphroditus when he arrives is meant not only to forestall criticism (at least of Epaphroditus when he arrives) but also to further promote them as examples for the Philippians to follow and heed. If Epaphroditus is both the bearer and reader of this letter, as 2:29–30 suggests, then Paul has closely linked the reception of the letter to the reception of Epaphroditus by discussing this co-worker here.

Third, this section strongly suggests that the networks of power were complex in the early Pauline communities. Local church leaders could send out their own "apostles" on specific missions of limited duration without Paul's knowledge or permission, and yet even these emissaries seem ultimately to have been under the authority of Paul, for he can send them back and give instructions about them. Some combination of pneumatic and hierarchical authority structures best describes the early church, and without doubt social factors also affected who was able and had the time for church service. One must not forget about Paul's ongoing itinerant co-workers such as Timothy. As Holmberg says, "Paul did have a staff of collaborators who lived, travelled and worked with him. They served, at least for a time, as his full-time assistants when they were entirely at his disposal enabling him to use his more trusted assistants as a distance medium for his own presence in his churches."[26] Thus, in the end we must distinguish the service of Timothy, probably Paul's most trusted ongoing co-worker, and that of Epaphroditus. The former must be seen as an extension of Paul's own ministry; the latter as an extension of the Philippians' participation in Paul's ministry, one who Paul feels needs to return and serve in the local church again.

Chapter Eight _____

The *Probatio* — 2:1–4:3

THE THIRD APPEAL:
PAUL VS. THE APPALLING DOGS — 3:1–4:1

In the first chapter of this discourse, Paul had already presented himself to his Philippian converts as an example of Christ-like attitude and actions. He now takes greater pains to present himself in this way by means of a contrast with some of his perennial opponents, those Jewish Christians bent on imposing the Mosaic law even on Paul's Gentile converts as a means of their "going on to perfection" and becoming fulfilled if not also full-fledged Christians.[1] This argument is somewhat more polemical in tone than the others, but it pales in comparison to the polemics in Galatians (or 2 Corinthians), perhaps because here it is part of a deliberative, not forensic, argument. It is possible to see the argument here as a *reprehensio*. According to Bloomquist, "Paul's first steps in the *reprehensio* are to establish the Philippian community's purity and, through *negatio* argumentation in 3:2–4a, to deny the same purity to his 'opponents' (see 3:2). This *tour de force* requires Paul's opponents to prove the validity of their own experience of being *en Christō*."[2] In other words, part of the rhetorical function of this argument is to lessen or negate any appeal the opponents and their lifestyle might have in the Philippians' eyes.

> Thus the key to understanding the *reprehensio* lies not in understanding who the opponents were but in understanding the rhetorical function of these opponents as not fulfilling the Christ type. The depiction of Timothy in

2:19–24 and Epaphroditus in 2:25–30 that prefaces the *reprehensio* can only be understood as an intentional, radical contrast with Paul's depiction of those who perish because of their dependence on flesh.[3]

I would argue instead that the main contrast in this rhetorical unit is between Paul himself and his perennial opponents, with negative and positive examples.

Paul is not defending his apostleship here. Nor is he discoursing on his background for its own sake; he mentions it only to indicate the extent and character of things he gave up when he became a Christian.[4] Note that the comparison in vv. 5–7 has to do with Paul's past, not with his present authority or credentials. He is modeling for his converts how they should react to the appeal to be circumcised and keep the Mosaic law. The aim of this entire argument is revealed in v. 17: "Be co-imitators of me, and watch that you are walking just as we have set the example."[5]

Here Paul alludes to all that he said in the previous two appeals about himself, Timothy, and Epaphroditus as examples, with Christ as the ultimate paradigm lying behind all these lesser models. If this advice is followed, then it will produce more unity in the congregation in Philippi for "the source of unity is found in living your lives as citizens . . . in a way worthy of the gospel of Christ."[6]

Watson is correct not to see the argument in this chapter as somehow a digression from the main flow of thought in the letter. Rather, it should be seen as the third main appeal for unitive behavior, using examples (both positive and negative) of the disposition (see especially v. 15) and behavior that produces such unity. The conclusion that chapter 3 is a digression has been drawn by some interpreters because too much weight has been placed on the few more polemical verses (2, 18, 19) to the neglect of the majority of the material in this appeal. Paul is making a positive point by means of comparison and contrast leading to the exhortation for the audience to be imitators of him and his co-workers, not of the evil workers. The theme announced in the *propositio* of the contrasting ends of true Christians and their opponents (1:28) comes to full development in 3:19–21, and the appeal to stand firm found first in 1:27 is reiterated and strengthened in 4:1.[7]

Thus, in chapter 3 Paul will build on what he said in chapter 2 about following the example of Christ and others. Here he will hold himself up as an example and will exhort his audience to emulate him and Christ according to the picture displayed in the Christ hymn in chapter 2. "The sequence of privilege-death-exaltation suggests such a connection, and this is confirmed by explicit verbal parallels: *hegeomai* (2:6; 3:7–8), *morphē* (2:7; *symmorphizō* 3:10), *heuriskō* (2:7; 3:9), *kyrios* (2:11; 3:8)."[8] Paul wishes to counteract other models of what the Christian life ought to look like that were or might be offered to the Philippians. Specifically, he is combating Judaizers, Jewish Christians who offered a very different sort of vision of the Christian life.

As Craddock stresses, v. 7 is a key to understanding the way Paul views his Jewish past:

> He does *not* say of his former life that it was in the loss column of the ledger, but rather that in his new way of reckoning, he counted gain as loss.... Paul does not say Judaism is worthless, that it is refuse... that intrinsically that way of life is of no value. What he is describing is his consuming desire to know Jesus Christ, to be in Christ... and for the surpassing worth of that, he *counts* gain as loss.... Paul does not toss away junk to gain Christ; he tosses away that which was of tremendous value to him.... There is absolutely nothing here remotely akin to the popular type of testimony that catalogs all the sins... that were tossed in the garbage can at conversion.... What Paul is saying is that Christ surpasses everything of worth to me. We need to keep in mind Paul's model in 2:6–11, the Christ who did not relinquish the low and base for something better, but who gave up all claim to equality with God in exchange for obedient service.[9]

In this section, Paul offers arguments that are in some respects strikingly similar to those in 2 Corinthians 11–13. It is not clear, however, how much these opponents had already affected or influenced the Philippians' thinking. It would appear that Paul's words are more a reminder than a corrective. Furthermore, this is apparently not the first time Paul has spoken to the Philippians about the Judaizers.

Translation

3:1 Well then my brothers and sister, rejoice in the Lord. It is no trouble to me to write the same thing to you [again], but (for) you a safeguard. **2**Consider [the example of] the dogs, consider the deceitful workers, consider the mutilators, **3**for we are the circumcision worshiping by the Spirit of God and glorifying Christ Jesus and not trusting in the flesh. **4**Although I have grounds [for boasting] even in the flesh, if some others think they have grounds in the flesh, I have more so: **5**in regard to circumcision an eighth day, from the race of Israel, the tribe of Benjamin, a Hebrew from Hebrews, with regard to the law a Pharisee, **6**with regard to zeal persecuting the church, with regard to righteousness (the sort found in the law), blameless. **7**[But] whatever was gain to me this I considered loss because of Christ. **8**But indeed I continue to consider all to be a loss because of the supreme value of knowing Christ Jesus my Lord, because of whom I have forfeited all things and I continue to consider them refuse in order to gain Christ **9**and be found in him, not having my own righteousness [the kind coming from the law] but rather the kind [coming] through the faithfulness of Christ, the from-God-righteousness [bestowed] upon the faith[ful], **10**those who know him and the power of his resurrection and the sharing in common of his sufferings, sharing conformity to his death, **11**if somehow I might reach unto the resurrection which comes from out of the dead.

12Not that I have already received,* or already reached perfection, but I continue pushing so also I might gain possession, seeing that I also have been possessed by Christ. **13**Brothers

---

Chapter 3 presents us with few serious textual problems. The most interesting is the addition in 3:12 of the phrase "or have already been justified" in p46, D, and a few other witnesses. This, however, represents a non-Pauline insertion, for Paul certainly does think he has already been justified in Christ.

[and sisters] I myself do not reckon to have arrived, but one thing [I do], forgetting the things behind, **14**but forging ahead to the things before, I continue pushing forward to the goal-marker unto the prize of the upward calling of God in Christ Jesus. **15**Whoever then of us is perfect, we may think this [way]. **16**If anyone thinks any differently, God will also reveal this to you, only let us keep in line in the stage we have reached.* **17**Be co-imitators of me, brothers [and sisters] and watch those who are living [accordingly], just as you have our example. **18**For many live whom many times I have spoken to you about, but now I speak also weeping — the enemies of the cross of Christ. **19**The end [of them] being destruction, their god the belly, and their glory in their shame, focusing on earthly things. **20**For our constituting government is in heaven, from which place we eagerly await a saviour Jesus Christ **21**who will transform the body of our humble state, sharing the form of his glorious body according to his dynamic working of his power, and he will subjugate all things to himself. **4:1**Therefore my beloved and longed for brothers [and sisters], my joy and crown, stand firm in the Lord, beloved.

Chapter 3 begins with one of the notes that most characterizes the whole epistle, the call to rejoice. Caird aptly says,

> Joy is a safeguard against the utilitarian attitude which judges people and things wholly by the use that can be made of them; and Christian joy, the exaltation of spirit that flows from acceptance of the free gifts of God's grace, is the best protection against the book-keeping mentality which assumes that every good thing must be a reward for virtue and offers no halfway house between smugness and a bad conscience.[10]

The Greek words *To loipon* need not have the meaning "finally," for they involve a resumptive particle, or an indication of changing gears, not necessarily of summing up, though they can be used for that as well. In 1 Corinthians 1:16, 4:2, 7:29, and

---

*In 3:16 a few later manuscripts add the phrase, "to think the same thing," but the shorter text has better support and is likely original.

2 Thessalonians 2:1, *loipon* means "and so," "well then," "more-over," or possibly "therefore." As M. E. Thrall puts it, there is clear evidence in the NT "that *loipon* in post-classical Greek could be used simply as a transitional particle, to introduce either a logical conclusion or a fresh point in the progress of thought."[11] It seems to have the latter function here. It is quite unnecessary to derive a whole partition theory on the basis of this one word.[12]

Paul adds that it does not bother him to repeat himself since he does so to safeguard or protect his converts in Philippi. He says essentially the same thing again at 3:18 about repeating himself, a point too little noted that suggests that we should see 3:1–2 and 3:18 as parallel discussions of the same subject, the Judaizers. The word "safeguard" tips us off that Paul is likely already alluding to what he is about to say concerning the "dogs." The word "repeat" may refer back to the mention of these folks in the *propositio* in 1:28 or possibly to Paul's having previously discussed these opponents with the Philippians, either orally or in some previous letter now lost.[13]

The verb *blepete* in v. 2 has played a significant role in the debate about the character of this material and deserves careful handling. It is usually translated "beware" with the implication that the "dogs" were currently dogging the steps of the Philippians. G. D. Kilpatrick argues that this verb, when followed by an accusative direct object, means "consider," not "beware," and points to texts like 1 Corinthians 1:26, "consider [*blepete*] your calling."[14] Perhaps even more apposite, since we are dealing with a discourse about examples, would be 1 Corinthians 10:18: "consider [*blepete*] Israel according to the flesh." If the latter translation is followed, then Paul may be saying no more than "consider the example of my perennial opponents as opposed to my example," without any implication that they are currently plaguing the Philippians.[15]

Against this being a *purely* hypothetical example that the Philippians have never been confronted with are two points: (1) 1:28 suggests *they* have encountered these opponents; and (2) Paul has apparently spoken to the Philippians about them previously. It seems likely that Paul is appealing to an example of opponents already familiar to the Philippians who perhaps have caused trouble in the past but are not necessarily troubling them at the moment this letter is being written. This would explain why they are not alluded to again in the concluding *peroratio* of the letter, as one would expect. It also explains how they can be used in a deliberative argument without more polemics than we actually find in this passage.

On Jewish lips *kunē* was a derisive term referring to the uncircumcised, hence unclean, people, including especially Gentiles (see Deut. 23:18; 2 Pet. 2:22; Rev. 22:14; and the handling of Exod. 22:31 in M. Ned. 4:3; M. Bek. 5:6). Paul, however, has cleverly changed the term to mean those who are insisting on circumcision. In other words, Paul is using the rhetorical device of irony. Notice the play on words between mutilators (*katatomē*) and circumcision (*peritomē*).[16] There may be an allusion to Leviticus 21:5 (LXX) in the former term, referring to the sort of incisions in or mutilations of human flesh that Moses prohibited.

Paul's basic complaint about these dogs is that they are evil workers; they seem to promise a sort of perfection for Christians if only they will fully obey the law, including stipulations concerning food and circumcision. This description of the opponents should be compared to how Paul describes his opponents in 2 Corinthians 11:13. The term "workers" suggests that these are rival missionaries, to be contrasted with Paul's faithful co-workers. The term may also suggest that Paul is mainly concerned that they are offering an aberrant view of Christian living, though this also entails some faulty theology on their part as well.

The reason this sort of view prompts such strong language from Paul is that it strikes at the heart of his gospel: justification is by grace through faith. Justification is not based on works of the law, but on the death of Christ on the cross. Hence Paul will go on to call these people enemies of the cross of Christ. Paul says that they are guilty of trusting in the flesh, in earthly things like food laws and circumcision, rather than in the gospel he preaches. He is even willing to go so far as to say that these people have as their ruling deity their stomach, by which he seems to mean that they are ruled not by a gospel of grace but by food laws. The reference to the fact that their glory is in their shame is likely a euphemism for nakedness, in particular, for the genitals. This would be an allusion to their insistence on circumcision.[17] In other words, neither of these metaphors forces the conclusion that Paul is discussing a different group of opponents (libertines?) in 3:19. It is possible then to produce a coherent interpretation of this passage on the assumption that Paul is referring to one set of opponents in this chapter, not two, as Koester ably argues.[18]

Are these people Christians or Jews?[19] Strongly against the theory that Paul is speaking about non-Christian Jews in Philippians 3[20] is the fact that we have here a deliberative argument contrasting one model of religious behavior with another that Paul believes his audience might actually be tempted to follow.[21] Unlike the case with Corinth, there is no good historical evidence that there was any significant Jewish presence in Philippi or any notable interest in Judaism on the part of Gentiles there. Acts 16:11–15 likely comports with this conclusion, for it suggests there was no synagogue or even a male quorum to form one in Philippi.[22]

The polemic about these "dogs" being enemies of the cross of Christ is fully effective only if they aspired to be followers of Christ in the first place. Furthermore, the real matter that decides the issue of who the opponents are is the one Lincoln brings to the fore.[23] Paul stresses that knowing Christ and being found in him is the only gain worth having, and this brings a whole new perspective on righteousness. This argument by no means would have countered, much less convinced, the opposition if they were simply Jews.

No, the opposition Paul has in mind, whether or not they are actually in Philippi when this letter was written, are those advocating a more dangerous blend of professing Christ and the law in such a way as to diminish the saving work of Christ. This means that despite all the boasting about Jewish qualities, which may even have included boasting about race, about being the real Israel, and about being perfect through obedience to the law, these opponents must also have to some degree professed Christ, or else Paul's argument is not to the point.

It would appear also that Paul envisions these opponents as guilty of an overrealized eschatology. They may have believed that the future resurrection was now and/or that perfection in some sense could be had in the present. To counter this Paul must make clear the future eschatological nature of both resurrection and perfection. Paul must contrast the "already" that he has in mind — which he says amounts to worshiping by the power of the Spirit and glorifying Christ, not trusting in human deeds of obedience to the law — with the "not yet" of resurrection and perfection.[24]

This passage is full of intentional irony, not unlike that in 2 Corinthians 11–13, with deliberate false boasting meant to shame the opposition, coupled with language meant to forestall or stop any boasting by anyone inclined to take the opposition's viewpoint. Paul first boasts of his Jewish pedigree and then turns around and says he now counts it as refuse or dung because of the surpassing worth of knowing Christ. In vv. 4–6 Paul lists those traits of which he could well have boasted, if he were to evaluate them from a human point of view. He can outdo his opponents in boasting about his Jewishness (note the "I more so").

If they boast of circumcision, he was circumcised on the day the OT required. He was a Jew among Jews by birth. Also he was a Hebrew from Hebrews. Now this may mean he came from people who spoke Hebrew (see Acts 6:11), or it may have a broader sense that he was no Hellenistic Jew but by culture had retained his pure Jewishness as had his parents. Probably the former is in view here.[25] Further, as a Benjaminite, Paul was named after the most illustrious member of that tribe, Saul, and the tribe of Benjamin was noted for remaining faithful to Judah.

In terms of the sort of righteousness one could have on the basis of obedience to the law, Paul says he was blameless. This is not to be confused with a claim to being perfect. It meant that he was not guilty of any violations according to Mosaic law. He could not be accused of any wrongdoing. As Marshall stresses, Paul is saying all of this from the point of view of his Pharisaic past; this is how he would have evaluated himself when he was a Pharisee. Of course, this would no longer be true, since he was no longer a Jew fully observant of the Mosaic requirements,[26] and in fact texts like 1 Corinthians 15:9 make clear that Paul as a Christian knew in retrospect that while a Pharisee he certainly was not without fault or blame in God's sight. How could he be when he was opposing God's chosen anointed one and his followers?

Nevertheless, it is important to stress that the upshot of Philippians 3:6 is that *prior* to his conversion there is no evidence that Saul saw himself as a guilt-ridden individual, even though he was persecuting some fellow Jews who were Christians. "We do not have in this text the portrait of a man at war with himself, crucified between the sky of God's expectations and the earth of his own paltry performance. Paul is not in this scene a poor soul standing with a grade of ninety-nine before a God who counts one hundred as the lowest passing grade."[27]

There is also no shred of evidence that Romans 7:14–25 describes how Paul *felt* about himself *prior* to his conversion to Christianity. That passage is more likely Paul's Christian reflection on the pre-Christian state.[28] It is only after the fact and after Damascus Road that Paul has remorse and regret about his behavior while still a Pharisaic Jew (see Gal. 1:13, 23; 1 Cor. 15:9; 1 Tim. 1:13).[29]

Were his opponents zealous? So was Paul, even to the point of persecuting the church. But Paul says all such things he now counts as *skubala*. This word can mean "muck," "spoiled food," "garbage" (see Sir. 27:4), or it can mean "dung."[30] It is possible that Paul is developing a consistent metaphor here. The things the "dogs" so value (that which makes one distinctively Jewish, including keeping kosher) is now to be reckoned as little more than dog food, decaying scraps, or refuse that would be thrown out and eaten by foraging canines.[31] If *skubala* means "dung" then the metaphor still may be being pursued and would refer to the food the human body could not use (excrement).[32] In any case, Paul is saying that such earthly things, however good in themselves, have been totally eclipsed by the value of knowing Christ. Indeed, such practices as keeping food laws can be a detriment to receiving salvation by grace through faith, if one uses them to make a claim on God. Better to count them as loss in order to be found in Christ.

In vv. 7ff. Paul uses an accounting metaphor. One is reminded of a ledger with credits and debits. The only thing to place on the credit side, Paul says, is knowing Christ and the power of his resurrection. Paul considered, and continues to consider, all other things as loss. Christ is the one supreme good, the one thing of supreme value. Paul says in v. 8 that he has lost everything as a result of his allegiance to Christ. This may have meant property, but more certainly he lost his Jewish friends, his high status in Judaism, and perhaps his wife.[33] Paul gave it all up to follow Christ. Under such circumstances, the idea of some Christian actually boasting about such things, which he had counted as loss in order to be faithful to Christ, can only cause revulsion in Paul. For him this amounted to a repudiation of the gospel and, in particular, of the cross of Christ.

In v. 9 we find the much controverted phrase *dia pisteos Christou*, literally "through the faith/fulness of Christ." I have argued that when one compares this verse to the close parallel in Romans 3:22 it leads to the conclusion that the reference here is not to Christian faith in Christ but Christ's faithfulness even unto death on the cross.[34] A variety of factors favor this rendering. First, we have already pointed out the numerous close verbal connections between the Christ hymn and the discussion in Philippians 3. This would simply be another example of such a link. Second, there is no doubt that the phrase that follows in 3:9b means "the from-God righteousness." Paul is discussing the means by which the believer obtains right-standing with God. Third, the natural rendering of *dia* here is *through*, not *in*. Fourth, the reference to Christian faith comes only at the end of this verse where we hear that this righteousness or right-standing is bestowed upon those of faith. An earlier reference to Christian faith would be quite superfluous, especially when the subject is the objective *source* of this righteousness: not from the law, but from the faithful acts of Christ. Finally, the whole drift of this letter is a matter of appealing to examples of godly faithfulness and sacrificial behavior that produce unity. Philippians 3:9 should be seen as furthering such an argument.[35]

The things of real value Paul lists in v. 10: knowing Christ (*gnōsis* likely means the knowledge that includes experience) and the power of his resurrection, which he can experience now in part. Note, however, that Paul also stresses that experiencing the resurrection "out from among the dead" comes only later. He also speaks of sharing in Christ's sufferings. Elsewhere he speaks of filling up Christ's suffering (Col. 1:24). He thus has a sense of having the honor of suffering with Christ for the same end and reason. This is part of what it means to be conformed to his death, not only inwardly but also outwardly. For Paul the "imitation of Christ" meant not just human choices and actions but also human experiences, often unavoidable ones, which God uses to conform one further to the image of Christ.

Verse 11 states what yet lies in the future, the hope of reaching the resurrection from out of the dead. Here Paul clearly envisions, as he does in 1 Corinthians 15, a resurrection of Christians from among the dead. This does not amount to a general resurrection of all the dead, probably because for Paul resurrection means being made like Christ in one's body, and he does not believe non-Christians or apostate Christians will receive that.[36] They will receive destruction, a fate that Paul says the Judaizers are also heading toward if they do not straighten out.

Verse 11 probably also shows that Paul does not count his own personal future resurrection as a foregone conclusion. The phrase "if possible" could be used here to counter the Judaizers who may have offered guarantees of salvation if one kept the Mosaic law. Paul's own view is that even those who have preached Christ could be disqualified if they did not remain in Christ and obey him (see 1 Cor. 9:27). Paul's basic view of salvation seems to have been that one is not eternally secure until one is securely in eternity. Until that time one must work out one's salvation in the context of the body of Christ, and this requires strenuous effort, hence the athletic metaphors here and elsewhere. "Trust in God's grace did not make Paul less active than the Judaizers but rather set him free now to run without watching his feet, without counting his steps, without competing with other servants of Christ."[37]

Thus, in v. 12 Paul turns to an athletic metaphor to show how hard he is striving toward the goal marker. The *skopos* was the marker at the finish line on which the runner set his sight and toward which he ran. In contrast to his opponents, Paul makes clear that he does not claim to have reached the goal or perfection, as his opponents apparently asserted they had. Paul is apparently concerned that there are some in Philippi who may have found the offer of reaching perfection in this life as plausible and appealing. Paul says this cannot be so because perfection means being completely conformed to the image of Christ and that takes: (1) a full life lived like Christ's, including suffering and dying like Christ, if one is so called; and (2) experiencing a resurrection like Christ's. Paul says he does not consider himself to have crossed the finish line and reached perfection. Perfection comes only when one is conformed both in one's behavior and in one's physical form to Christ, exchanging a weak, perishable, inglorious body for one that is the opposite (see 1 Cor. 15:42–50).[38]

"Christ has already taken full possession of Paul; Paul in turn wants full possession of Christ."[39] He wishes to know Christ in a way that does not involve seeing through a glass darkly, as is the case for all believers in this life. Full communion comes only when Christ returns and full conformity to Christ's image is possible.

Thus Paul is forgetting all that is past, including the assets he accumulated as a Pharisaic Jew. He is not looking over his shoulder, much less looking back with longing. Rather, like a good runner he has his eye fixed on the goal and the prize that results. Paul explains that the prize amounts to the "upward" or "heavenly" calling of God. This probably is an allusion to the calling out by the judge of the winner's name or perhaps his being called up to the *bema,* or judge's seat, to receive the wreath. Thus Paul in v. 15 says with irony that those among the Philippians who are truly "perfect" will think as Paul has been urging them, not like the Judaizers.

Here Paul likely uses the term *teleioi* in the sense of "mature." He is in effect saying that those who are truly mature (*teleios*) will know that they have not yet reached perfection (*teleios*), because they have not reached the goal (*telos*) of complete con-formity to Christ's image, including conformity in one's physical form. A "perfect" self-understanding for Christians always entails knowing that they have not yet reached perfection in this life, because perfection means being as completely like Christ as any mere mortal can be.

Paul is quite confident of his point of view. For him it is not just a matter of opinion. He says that if any think otherwise God will enlighten them about the matter. The crucial thing in this life is not claiming a false perfection that is less than full confor-mity to Christ's image but rather keeping in line with the stage one has reached in the Christian life. One is held responsible for living up to the level of Christian maturity one has already obtained.

As Marshall points out, this appeal in v. 16 to go on liv-ing up to what they have obtained "incidentally suggests that the danger had not yet corrupted the church."[40] Paul appears to be forestalling or reminding about a potential problem here, not an actual one, and in the main the opponents are brought into the discussion as negative examples, not as real pariahs already plaguing Philippi. Accordingly, excessive mirror-reading and speculations about what beliefs and practices the Philippi-ans' opponents had already corrupted are not in order here.

For Paul, as his earlier autobiographical remarks make clear, keeping kosher and being circumcised would be a step backward in the Christian life, and he does not want his converts to take up what he himself left behind and now reckoned in the loss column. In v. 17 we have a straightforward appeal for the Philip-pians to imitate Paul, or for them all together to be co-imitators (*sun* compound) of Paul, making a collective effort. They are to live following Paul's example.

The call to imitation was a common one for teachers, includ-ing both rhetoricians and philosophers, to make in antiquity, for modeling was believed to be one of the most effective ways to be educated. Such calls to imitation often assumed a very special and close relationship between the mentor and his followers. This was a technique especially common in deliberative rheto-ric, where the orator is trying to persuade his audience about their future course of action. There was an additional reason why the call for imitation was crucial in early Christianity, especially when dealing with Gentile converts. "To show them how to walk, those first generation believers, with no precedent or history, with no NT, with few preachers and most of them itinerant, struggling as a minority in a pagan culture, no better textbook could be offered than the lives of those who stood before them as leaders."[41]

It may be added that such appeals and examples must have been made all the more urgent if the rival missionaries were appealing to the Hebrew Scriptures as an authority for Christians. Paul had to explain how they were not to be heeded without treating the OT as if it were wrong or misleading. He does this by a hermeneutical move that is fully explained only in Galatians 3–4. There he indicates that the Mosaic covenant with its law and regulations was a good gift from God, but binding only on an earlier stage of salvation history and an earlier group of God's people, which did not include Gentiles in any significant numbers. Since Christ had died on the cross the situation with God's people had changed.

Now, right-standing with God was *obtained* through faith in Christ because of the faithfulness of Christ even unto death on the cross; it was not *maintained* by keeping the Mosaic law. Christians had reached a stage in the life of God's people where striving to keep the Mosaic law would be an act of immaturity, of going backward rather than forward in God's plan for God's people (see Gal. 3:23–26).

Even if the Judaizers were arguing only that one needed to add Moses to Christ to be perfect, Paul had to reject such a gospel, because it meant imposing the Mosaic approach to Gentiles (that they must become converts or at least proselytes to Judaism in order to be acceptable to God) on those who had right-standing with God *already*, simply by means of Christ's faithfulness and their faith in his death, resurrection, and subsequent Lordship (see Phil. 2:6–11).

Paul is extremely upset about his opponents, but he also weeps for them. Because of their ideas and practice of the Christian life, they have become enemies of the cross, the latter being the very essence of Paul's gospel. If obeying the Mosaic law is necessary for salvation, then *ipso facto* Christ's death on the cross was not sufficient to provide that same salvation.

In v. 20 Paul offers an alternative to earthly glorying in things like food laws and circumcision.[42] Here again we have a real problem in translating the hapax legomenon *politeuma*. Its possible meanings are: (1) colony, though it is unlikely to mean this here, since Paul would surely have said a colony of heaven, not a colony *in* heaven; (2) commonwealth; (3) state; (4) constitution; and (5) citizenship. This last meaning is not well attested in Paul's day. It normally means something like state or commonwealth as a dynamic constituting force regulating its citizens, and seems comparable in force to the term *basileia* when it means a kingly reign rather than a realm.[43]

What Paul is seeking to say is that a Christian's ruler (Christ) is in heaven, and the ruling principles for their behavior are derived from heaven and Christ, including Christ's example. This is in contrast to those whose ruling principles are what Paul calls earthly or fleshly. "To the Philippians the *politeuma* was in Rome ... [but] the apostle makes the claim about the *politeuma* of Christians ... [that].... Their state and constitutive government is in heaven and they are to reflect this rule in every respect."[44] This commonwealth is not yet fully manifested on earth, of course, but Paul believes that Christians are already citizens of it and should live accordingly, imitating the behavior of the Christ and his earthly emissaries.

It has often been asserted that Paul may be quoting part of a hymn in v. 21. It is more likely that he is reflecting on the hymn he already quoted in 2:6–11. In 3:20–21 there are a variety of striking verbal echoes to 2:6–11,[45] for example, the close juxtaposition of "Lord" with "Jesus Christ" and the pattern of transformation from a lowly to an exalted and glorious condition. Christ's history is the believer's destiny.

Here is the only place, apart from once in Ephesians (if it is by Paul), that Paul calls Christ "savior." He does this perhaps to stress that salvation is not complete here and now before the savior comes and finally transforms believers. I would suggest, however, that Paul has also chosen to use the word *sōtēr* along with *politeuma* in order to appeal effectively to those who resided in a Roman colony; they would be proud of their Roman citizenship and would be familiar with the use of the term *sōtēr* with reference to the emperor. There is also a further reason why he may have used the term. When in 42 B.C.E. Octavian conferred on Philippi the privilege of having a Roman form of government, it was granted the right to be governed as if it were a city on Italian soil. Its administration reflected that of Rome's in nearly every respect. The Philippians then would have a very good idea what it meant to live by ruling principles that originated from afar.[46]

It is important to notice, however, that Paul uses *politeuma* in a transferred sense. The use of this terminology here is not to emphasize the Philippians' civic responsibility, any more than the use of *politeuesthe* in 1:27 was. Rather, the language of civic responsibility and affiliation "has been transferred to the corporate life of the church" to make clear that Christ, Christian principles, and Christ's people have a higher and prior claim on their lives.[47] This is so because they have a higher and more powerful *sōtēr* who will come to save them not merely from Rome but from heaven itself. Earthly citizenship and the benefits rulers can convey are overshadowed by those that Christ conveys and will convey to believers.

A Closer Look: The Emperor as *Sōtēr* (Savior) and Christ as Servant

As A. D. Nock demonstrated, the term *sōtēr* was used widely in the Greco-Roman world of both divine and human savior figures; it came to be especially used of the emperor after the time of Augustus, and specifically of deceased emperors who had been divinized in the cult. Thus, for example, Germanicus in 19 C.E. in an edict to the citizens of Alexandria says, "I altogether deprecate acclamations of yours...which belong to the level of divinity [*isotheous*], for they are suitable only for him who is really *sōtēr* and *euergetes* [benefactor] of the whole human race, that is my father [Augustus], and for his mother...."[48] Later emperors were not reluctant to accept the title while living, and Domitian went so far as to allow himself to be acclaimed *Deus et Dominus nos-*

ter (God and our Lord). Nock sums up: *"Sōtēr,* while most often used of emperors, was at times formally applied to local dignitaries and to Imperial functionaries, in a manner which indicates that it was not felt to be excessive or invidious."[49] It could even be used in a very mundane way to refer to the work of magistrates who had "saved" a city from ruin after an earthquake or famine, perhaps through obtaining or donating a monetary gift.[50]

It *could be* imperial eschatology rather than overrealized Judaizing eschatology that Paul is here counteracting or seeking to critique with his singular use of *sōtēr* coupled with *politeuma;* thus it may be important to see the emperor-as-savior figure lurking in the background of this discussion. Marshall puts it this way: "The imagery is that of a visiting head of state, here probably regarded as a conqueror or invader who delivers those of his people who have fallen into captivity in a foreign land."[51]

The presence of the imperial cult in Philippi seems clear enough from the inscriptional evidence,[52] and in fact there were both imperial and local aristocracies that participated in this cult in Philippi. One example, probably from the first century c.e., is that of C. Oppius Montanus, honored as *flamen* and patron of Philippi (*Corpus Inscriptionum Latinarum* 3:7340). As the first century progressed, there was greater and greater stress on the imperial cult and its propaganda about the emperor-as-savior when cities, especially Roman colony cities, sought to enhance their ties with Rome and thus their access to its resources and aid.

The salvation that the emperor was believed to provide by means of the *Pax Romana* included the blessings of safety, health, and wealth, blessings that chiefly benefited the upper echelons of society, including Roman citizens in particular.[53] Paul was offering a very different sort of savior figure, one who was for everyone, even those in the lowest status in society, even those who endured the status and punishment of slaves (crucifixion).

It is important to note that Paul's words would not likely be taken to indicate some revolutionary program against the Empire, however, because Paul stresses that the transformation of the physical order, including that of human bodies, comes only at the return of Christ from heaven. Nevertheless, one must not overlook the social component of Paul's thought here. He may be seeking to unify the Christian community in Philippi by urging a certain relativizing of and detachment from the values of imperial eschatology and Roman citizenship and an adherence to more specifically Christian values. These Christian values do not include simply equating salvation with health, wealth, and safety. To the contrary, because of Christ's example the experience of salvation incorporates a positive evaluation of suffering and involves the ability to do with or without various material goods, even good health (see Phil. 4:11–12).

When the form of the world is passing away and eschatological salvation is already being provided in Christ, it becomes impossible in Paul's view to place ultimate value on things that in the end are temporary. It is a mistake to equate Paul's vision of salvation with a purely spiritual and non-social one. Paul's ultimate solution to the human dilemma is not escape to heaven. It is just that Paul does not believe the material transformation and re-creation of this world will transpire in any full sense before Christ returns. Before that time the Christian should concentrate on reformation within the social structure of the community of faith and on proclamation of the Good News outside the community.

One social effect of reading and applying Paul's Philippian discourse would be a change in understanding of status and status indicators. If people like Christ and Paul indicate how honor is obtained and what amounts to status (namely, being approved by God at the eschaton), this surely must cause a transvaluation of normal Roman values. Furthermore, if the examples of Christ, Paul, and his co-workers as servants of God were heeded, then there would be a leveling effect on the community, which also would promote unity in the *ekklēsia*.

Paul operates basically with a faith in the gospel concept that the lowly and servants will be exalted in due course by God and should now be honored in the community as models of proper Christ-like behavior. The Christian community was to provide a visible example of life lived according to kingdom values and as an alternative to many of the values of the larger society. It seems, in other words, to offer in microcosm entrance into the future world, but only in part.

In a stimulating discussion of burial associations and *koina,* or clubs, set up for and by foreigners and traveling tradesmen and tradeswomen in various Roman cities, G. H. R. Horsley suggests that Philippians 3:20 should be read in light of the fact that members of such clubs had what virtually amounted to a separate citizenship, with special rights, privileges, honors, prizes, and benefits that did not apply to those not members of the group.[54] One may further add that these groups, being microcosms of society, were often socially diverse, as was early Christianity, and even slaves had status and rights in the club that were not theirs in the outside world.[55]

I want to stress that Paul's eschatological outlook shapes how he views the social realities of the early Christian community in various ways. Paul's already-and-not-yet eschatology required of his converts an interesting balancing act between: (1) rejection and acceptance of some of the larger cultural values; (2) inclusivity and exclusivity of community, entailing open, yet somewhat clear, ethical and theological boundaries for the community; (3) de-enculturation and yet transformation of the larger culture, at least as one dealt with individuals who were being led to Christ.

These are the normal tensions inherent in a missionary religion with an eschatological world view that nonetheless wishes to maintain a clear sense of its identity. It cannot simply become a world-denying sect that withdraws, like the Qumran community, but on the other end of the spectrum it also must not become simply assimilated to the values of the larger culture. It is part counter-culture and, to the extent it affirmed larger cultural values, part subculture.

Paul's vision included partial transformation of society in the Christian community in the present, and in the world as a whole when Christ returns later. There were many values that were for Paul nonnegotiable, however, and perhaps the chief of these was that only Christ in any full sense could be called *sōtēr*, much less savior of the world.

Christ is eagerly awaited, for he will transform this humble body into a glorious one. Paul is convinced this will transpire because Christ has the even greater power to subjugate all things to himself. Even rebellious human flesh will finally be transformed and submit with all the rest of creation to Christ's reign when Christ returns. It should be abundantly clear from this passage that, even late in life, Paul still strongly holds to a future eschatological conclusion of salvation here on earth, not simply in heaven without a body.[56]

Paul concludes his argument in this portion of his letter with the word of exhortation found in 4:1: "so then stand firm." Paul is saying, "We have a great hope in front of us; let us not sell it short by buying a bill of goods that suggests perfection is something less than the total transformation of the person, even in the body. Only this is full and final salvation: the complete conformity to Christ's image, not just in spirit and character but also in the body. This alone is true perfection."

In finishing this appeal, Paul twice calls the Philippians his beloved (*agapētoi*), speaking of what they are to him now, but he also calls them his crown and joy, speaking of what they will be at the day of Christ's return.[57] Paul envisions a grand celebration, perhaps like that at the end of the Olympic games, where the victors are given their wreaths and there is much rejoicing over what has been accomplished by those who have run and successfully finished their races. This verse alone should be sufficient to make clear that Paul does not think the Philippians have already succumbed in any significant way to the ploys and pleas of Judaizing Christian missionaries, but he is warning them solemnly to continue to stand firm, for listening to the Judaizers could only further divide the congregation in Philippi.[58]

Chapter Nine

The *Probatio* — 2:1–4:3

THE FOURTH APPEAL:
WOMEN AT ODDS — 4:2–3

Though the fourth appeal is exceedingly brief, it is obvious that Paul felt it crucial to close the argument section of the letter with a final appeal for two important women in the Philippian congregation to be united.[1] While it is probably saying too much to suggest that all of what has gone before was leading up to these verses,[2] nevertheless the brevity of this argument can be attributed in part to the fact that Paul assumes that these women will have heard and learned from the earlier appeals for self-sacrificial behavior that produces unity. The general guidelines referred to earlier now receive a quite specific and concrete application.

The argument of Watson that 4:2–3 should be seen as part of the closing *peroratio* is not convincing.[3] Paul is not simply repeating concerns dealt with earlier in the letter. Rather, he is dealing with one particular example of divisive behavior that threatens the congregation, building on some of the earlier advice. The *peroratio,* with its repetition of earlier themes, begins at 4:4 with the announcement again of the dominant appeal to rejoice. Furthermore, as C. J. Bjerkelund shows, it is normal in Paul's discourses to take the *parakalō* ("appeal," "urge," "encourage") as a sign of a new appeal;[4] in 4:2 we have a twofold use of *parakalō,* indicating the importance of this appeal. What these verses make clear is that Paul's earlier arguments were not purely hypothetical or simply attempts to forestall future problems. There were real examples of dissension in Philippi that required attention and guidance from Paul.

Translation

4:2I appeal to Euodia and I appeal to Syntyche to think the same in the Lord. **3**Yes, I also ask you, loyal yokefellow, assist these women who have struggled together with me in the [work of the] gospel, with Clement also and the rest of my co-workers, whose names are in the book of life.

There are no major textual problems in these verses.

There are various signs that these women are leaders in the Philippian congregation.[5] First, it is unlikely that Paul would attempt to interfere in a private disagreement in a public letter like this one. Rather, Paul is concerned because these women are setting a bad example for the congregation; because of their status and potential effect on the Philippian congregation Paul must correct this problem in a public letter meant to be read aloud before the congregation.

Second, Paul calls these women his co-workers, a term found only thirteen times in the NT, twelve in Paul's letters; it is not used by Paul of believers in general, but of those involved in the missionary or evangelistic work of the gospel. This is especially clear from a text like 1 Corinthians 16:16, 18, where Paul urges the Corinthians to submit to co-workers such as Stephanas (see 1 Cor. 3:9; 1 Thess. 3:2; Rom. 16:3, 9, 21; Phil. 2:25; Phlm. v. 24; 2 Cor. 1:24; 8:23). This is a term reserved for various early Christian leaders. It must be stressed that "Paul makes no slur upon their leadership; rather he praises them for having labored side by side with Clement and himself. His concern is not with the women's role but with the trouble the disagreements could cause the congregation."[6]

Third, the phrase "they fought together alongside of me in the gospel" ranks these women along with Clement and other male disciples as having a hands-on role in the promotion of the gospel. The verb *sunathleō*, used of gladiators who fought side by side, is yet another term drawn from athletic terminology.[7] The suggestion of F. X. Malinowski that this alludes to their defense of Paul during his initial missionary work in Philippi in the 40s is plausible. Perhaps 1 Thessalonians 2:2 bears adequate testimony to this occasion: "we had already suffered and been shamefully treated at Philippi, as you know...." In his attempt to deny that this passage implies that these women had anything to do with the proclamation of the gospel, Malinowski overlooks the fact that this is not all Paul has to say about these women. They are his co-workers along with Clement and as such they did more than struggle on Paul's behalf on that one occasion when suffering was involved.[8] In fact, the other use of this same verb is found in the *propositio* in 1:27, where we are told of those who fight side by side for the faith of the gospel, which surely implies some sort of sharing of the faith, even in the face of opposition.

It is very likely that these women were not patronesses, but leaders and proclaimers of the word, those who struggled in the gospel with Paul. It is possible that the particular dispute Paul is trying to mediate concerns who would get to be Paul's patron or who could outdo the other in generosity. The text is not sufficiently clear to draw a firm conclusion.

We should bear in mind that we are told in Acts 16 that the congregation in Philippi was begun with the conversion of a businesswoman who apparently had been some kind of adherent to Judaism before converting to Christianity. It is not out of the realm of possibility that Luke in Acts 16 is referring to a Lydian woman, not a woman named Lydia, which has led to the conjecture that one of these two women mentioned by name in Philippians 4:2–3 is that same woman.[9] We now have inscriptional evidence for Lydia as a personal name (in this case Julia Lydia of Sardis), however, and so the conjecture is probably wrong.[10] Equally unprovable but just barely possible is the suggestion that the Greek word *syzygos* is a proper name rather than a term meaning yokefellow. There is no evidence in the relevant sources of such a name. What is clearer is that this third party, who has been asked to intercede, is a male, as the gender of the word "loyal" makes apparent. Perhaps the least unreasonable conjecture is that this phrase refers to Epaphroditus, the bearer of this letter, as the one called upon to help solve this dilemma.[11] It is helpful to look at this text in the larger context of women and their roles in Greco-Roman society in the provinces and in particular in Macedonia, which had a long history of women of high and/or royal status assuming prominent positions in society.

Roman and Macedonian Women of Power, Privilege, and Status

It has long been recognized by classical and NT scholars that many women in Macedonia from the Hellenistic period onward had considerable prominence and influence. The comment of W. W. Tarn and G. T. Griffith is typical: "They played a large part in affairs, received envoys, and obtained concessions from them for their husbands, built temples, founded cities, engaged mercenaries, commanded armies, held fortresses, and acted on occasion as regents or even co-rulers."[12] The inscriptional evidence reveals that there were women who founded clubs and were actively involved in various social organizations (*Inscriptiones Graecae* 329 [1898] 12:3, 80). This was the legacy of the Hellenistic period in regard to women and their roles.

When we turn to the Roman period and deal with women living in a city within a Roman colony, additional discussion is required. First, Roman women were normally called by their family's *cognomen* and had no personal name to use in public.[13] The name of the two women mentioned in Philippians 4:2 occurs elsewhere in the inscriptional evidence, but there is no evidence at all of male equivalents of this name, so we may be sure that two *women* with Greek names are referred to here.[14] This suggests they are not of Roman extraction, but rather are from Macedonian or at least Greek families. There were numerous prominent Macedonian families involved in all levels of society in Philippi and elsewhere from which these women could have come.[15] Nevertheless, Roman conventions in regard to women and their roles would have been dominant in Philippi in the mid-first century C.E. What then do we know about Roman women's roles in the provinces?

A. J. Marshall deals with this subject at some length.[16] He shows that various women owned provincial estates and were well off and also that the wives of Roman provincial officials were often honored in the inscriptions and took roles in various of the religious cults.[17] "A large proportion of Roman women resident in the provinces were of freedman stock, and the more wealthy among them would retain the interest of the male members of the Roman family to whom they owed their freedom and whose legal wards they were."[18] Perhaps more germane is the evidence of Greek women with Roman citizenship who held high civic office and were priestesses in the imperial cult in Asia.[19] In this environment it is no surprise to find women of high status playing prominent roles in early Christian congregations in the provinces. It was money and social status that normally secured such roles including religious roles for women in society at large,[20] and these seem to have been factors in the cases of both men and women who assumed leadership roles in early Christianity as well.

This is not to say that all roles were open to women in the provinces. The structure of Roman society was highly patriarchal even during the Empire, when the status and power of women was on the rise,[21] but the point of importance for us is that with the absence of a strong Jewish presence in Philippi, and with the various religious roles available to women, especially those of higher status in pagan cults, female converts to Christianity in such a place would naturally expect to assume some prominent roles in this new Eastern religion.[22] The evidence in Philippians 4 and elsewhere indicates that these expectations were not ill-founded.

It is interesting to note that in Greek and Roman oratory it was common not to mention women by name, unless they were either very notable or very notorious.[23] One would suspect that this too indicates that Euodia and Syntyche were women of status and of great importance for the congregation in Philippi.[24] One must ask, What sort of woman had the time, resources, or freedom to struggle side by side with Paul on behalf of the gospel? Women of status are likely candidates, and perhaps single women or more well-to-do women with considerable power in their own families who could count on their servants to take care of most of the domestic responsibilities (see Acts 16:15). Early Christianity was socially diverse, and Philippians 4:2–3 is further testimony to this fact.

What is critical for our discussion is that Paul nowhere hints that he wishes these women to stop assuming roles as his co-workers. Rather, he wants them to stop quarreling so that they may get on with their ministries and not contribute to disunity in the Philippian congregation.

Two further points are worth considering. It is possible that these two women were leaders and hostesses in two different house churches, and Paul was worried about the sort of factionalism between house churches that seems to have existed in Corinth.[25] Perhaps they were among the *episkopoi* to whom Paul felt a need to refer in the opening address in Philippians 1:1.[26] "Most likely . . . what we have here is not a personal quarrel...but rather a substantive division within the church leadership which from the very beginning consisted largely of faithful women."[27]

Whatever the character of the disagreement between these two women, it would appear from the closing phrase in 4:3 that Paul does not think that their dispute is so serious that it affects their salvation. With others they are written in the book of eternal life (see Dan. 12:1; 1QM 12:3; Luke 10:20; Heb. 12:23; Rev. 3:5, 13:8, 17:8, 20:15). The issue here then is social discord, not soteriological debate or status.[28]

When Paul draws on expressions from earlier in the letter about laboring side by side (1:27) or being of the same mind (2:2), he is expecting these women to be astute and mature enough Christians to glean the proper lessons from the earlier material.[29] That such a direct exhortation to individuals in a group communication is virtually unprecedented in Paul's letters (but cf. Col. 4:17) attests to the importance of these women and Paul's concern that they could make the general appeal for unity in this letter of no effect unless they too accepted its lessons. He even asks Clement, and perhaps others by implication, to intercede to make sure that these co-workers once again contribute to the concord, not the discord, in Philippi.

Chapter Ten

The *Peroratio* — 4:4–20

DIVISION I:
"VIRTUE AS A NECESSITY" — 4:4–9

It is not uncommon for a *peroratio* to have two divisions, as this one does. The two basic functions of the *peroratio* are to reprise the main themes of the letter, which is the function of 4:3–9, and to create *pathos,* that is, the deeper emotions, in the audience, which is the function of 4:10–20. The former section is called the *repetitio,* the latter the *adfectus* (see Cicero *Inv.* 1.52–56; Quintilian *Inst. Or.* 6.1.1–55). The latter is usually further divided into a section in which one seeks to create negative feelings in the audience for the opponents and a final section where one seeks to create positive feelings toward oneself. Paul does not mention the opponents at all in either section of the *peroratio,* a fact that strongly suggests that they were not currently in Philippi troubling his converts. Though Paul feels strongly about the Judaizers, in this letter they serve the function of being (1) a negative example, mentioned directly only in 3:2, 18, 19 in a contrast with Paul, and (2) a reminder by the apostle to his audience of the way *not* to live out the implications of the faith. Philippians 1:28 likely suggests that the Judaizers had troubled the Philippians in the past (they were both Paul's and the Philippians' opponents), and perhaps Paul worried they might trouble them again in the not too distant future. The apostle believed that to be forewarned was to be forearmed.

In the first division of the *peroratio* we see the repetition of the theme of joy and rejoicing (v. 4). In v. 5a gentleness or forbearance (*epieikes*) is urged in a way not unlike what we find

110

in 2:1-3. This term is difficult to translate and has the general sense of meeting someone halfway — a good summary of the appeal of this whole letter for unity.[1] In v. 5b the reference to the nearness of the Lord is followed by the exhortation to pray (v. 6), which reprises the themes of the *exordium* in 1:3-11. "Most importantly, vv. 5-7 reiterate the proposition of 1:27-28 that forbearance and striving for the gospel are necessary because they are a witness in light of the parousia, and that the Philippians need not fear or be anxious because God is with them (cf. 2:12-13)."[2] Finally vv. 8-9 remind us of the appeal to character found in 2:3, 14-15, and elsewhere in the discourse.

Translation

[4]Rejoice in the Lord always. Again I say, rejoice. [5]Let your sweet reasonableness be known to everyone. The Lord is near. [6]Do not be anxious, but in all things pray and petition, with thanksgiving make your requests known to God. [7]And the peace of God which surpasses all understanding will stand sentry over your hearts and your thoughts in Christ Jesus.

[8]In addition then brothers [and sisters], whatever is true, whatever is honorable, whatever is right, whatever is pure, whatever is admirable, whatever is noble, if there is any virtue and if there is anything praiseworthy, [continuously] ponder[3] these things, [9]which you learned and received and heard and saw in me, practice, and the God of peace is with you.

Paul, as he draws the letter to a close, returns once more to the theme of joy at 4:4. As D. Ezell notes, this sudden shift from the focus of 4:3 indicates that we are at the beginning of a new subsection of the letter.[4] It should be noted that Paul does not say "rejoice because of all circumstances" but "rejoice in the Lord always." Paul believes that the primary and abiding source of joy for Christians comes from the presence of Christ in their lives, *not* from circumstances. If one has that source of joy, circumstances cannot take it away; indeed it can exist even in spite of negative circumstances.

The suggestion that *chairete* means "farewell" rather than or in addition to "rejoice" is surely made doubtful by the addition of the word *pantote*. What would "farewell in the Lord always" mean?[5] As Marshall says, the context here is a reprise of the letter's instructions, and greetings at this point do not suit such a context.[6]

The word *epieikes* is an important one. It is related to the word *eikos*, which means "reasonable." Aristotle contrasted this word with the idea of strict justice (*Nicom. Ethics* 5.10). It means something like magnanimity, referring to a person of compassionate nature who is willing to be loving above and beyond what is strictly fair. It amounts to showing concern and respect for the integrity of others and giving them the benefit of the doubt. In other words, it is the sort of quality necessary if there is to be unity among a diverse group of people. Wisdom of Solomon 2:19 suggests that it is an essential trait of a godly person, not merely of a judge or ruler. More importantly, in 2 Corinthians 10:1, where it is coupled with the term "meekness," Paul uses this very term to describe the character of Christ.

In v. 5 we also have the phrase "the Lord is *eggus* [near]." The term *eggus* can be used to mean nearness in space or time. As I have argued, the clue to interpreting this verse is to read it in tandem with v. 6 and to consider both in light of the Psalms.[7] When Paul thinks about prayer, he quite naturally reflects back on the prayer and praise book of the Hebrew Scriptures, the Psalms. Paul likely has in mind Psalm 145:18–19: "The Lord is near to those who call upon him." Further, Psalm 34:17–18 speaks of the righteous calling on the name of the Lord and further says, "The Lord is near to the brokenhearted" (see Ps. 119:151).[8] In other words, one must pick up the echo from the Psalms to properly understand Paul's meaning in vv. 5–6.

On other grounds as well, it is unlikely that Paul means the Lord is temporally near. For one thing *eggus*, when it is used elsewhere in the sense of temporal nearness, refers to a thing or an event, not a person, being near.[9] Thus, I conclude that Paul is counting on at least some of his audience being aware of the larger allusion to the Psalms and reminding them that the Lord is near and hears the prayers of the saints. Because of this Christians should not be anxious; instead of anxiety Christians should devote themselves to prayer.

Paul indicates that the Shalom of God comes to those who make known their prayers (*proseuchē*, a general word for prayer), petitions (*deēsei*, a more specific word), and requests (*aitēmata*, a word suggesting the content, not the form, of prayer). Note, too, that these prayers are to be offered with thanksgiving. The Christian who prays with a thankful heart, the one who bears in mind the past mercies and answers God has provided, prays in the right spirit. In Paul's view there is much to be said, not merely for praying, but for praying in the right spirit or frame of mind.[10] In this section Paul has used four different words for prayer, but this variety is for stylistic effect; it is not an attempt to identify four distinct types or elements of prayer. Only the term *eucharistia* (thanksgiving) refers to something specific here.[11]

Paul goes on to say that this peace of God that comes to believers is not an absence of anxiety; rather, it is the very assurance of God brought by the divine presence in their midst. Interestingly, he also says that this peace will stand watch over (or guard) the believers' hearts and minds, presumably protecting them from unnecessary worry or concerns. Paul is drawing on a military metaphor. "Since the city of Philippi was guarded by a Roman garrison at the time, the metaphor would have been easily understood and appreciated by the readers."[12] The future verb tense of *phrourēsei* suggests a sure promise, not a wish that is being expressed here.[13]

The term *huperexousa* means something that surpasses or exceeds something else. The key phrase may mean that God's peace surpasses all human mental capacity to grasp, or that God's peace surpasses our own mental efforts to provide for our own peace and security. In either case, Paul believes that it "is not only the peace of God but the God of peace...who will overshadow us with [divine] care."[14]

Throughout this passage and especially in vv. 8–9 it is important to remember two things. First, while Paul is not at all averse to borrowing terms and ideas from Greco-Roman moral discussions, he makes these terms his own, and the paradigms he holds up for his audience are always Christian or, in cases like

Abraham, Jewish. He would not extol a virtue that he thought
was inconsistent with the character of Christ or with living a
Christian life.[15] Second, it happens, however, that various of the
virtues Paul extols as characteristic of the Christian life are by
no means exclusively Christian. Virtue should be recognized and
appreciated wherever one finds it, even if the moral exemplars
are exclusively Jewish or Christian ones in Paul's letters. The
point of these observations is that Paul recognizes that virtue
is not the exclusive provenance of the Christian community, just
as he recognizes that the church and the world share some common moral ground. The moral boundaries of the church do not
exclude the world at every point; rather, there is some overlap in
concerns, views, ethics. Paul's remark in Romans 2:14 — "When
Gentiles, who do not possess the law, do instinctively what the
law requires, these . . . are a law unto themselves" — is not a purely
hypothetical statement.

What is significant about Paul's handling of this matter is not
that he draws on prior discussions of virtue and honor, but that
he believes that the example of Christ has something unique
and essential to add to such discussions, indeed that Christ is
the context in which one truly exegetes such terms. Thus, when
these virtues are discussed in the context of the call to emulate Christ or Paul or other positive Christian examples, the
combination of such terms placed in the matrix of the overshad-
owing image of the life and character of Christ provides a new
application and sometimes gives a new sense to such common
Greco-Roman terms.

This is especially clear in Paul's discussion of humility and
the pattern of Christ's life in Philippians 2, where the term
tapeinophrosunē takes on various positive connotations in the
Christian community, connotations it did not normally have in
other contexts. Paul does not merely borrow the discourse of
the Greco-Roman moralists nor does he simply tack it on to an
otherwise Judaeo-Christian discussion.[16] Rather, he incorporates
such language into his own thought world and makes it serve
his own Christian ends.

Thus, Philippians 4:4, 8-9 reflects clearly Paul's willingness
to draw on a variety of sources to create his own Christian dis-

course. This discourse would sound familiar to both Jew and Greek alike in some respects, until it became clear in the very first argument in Philippians 2 that the key to understanding Paul's rhetoric was a certain crucified manual worker from Galilee whom Paul believed God had raised from the dead, established as Lord, and set forth as *the* supreme example of virtue and true character for all, both Jew and Gentile. At this point, it becomes clear that we have gone beyond and in some sense against what someone like Musonius Rufus meant when he said:

> In general, of all creatures on earth humans alone resemble [*mimema*] God and have the same virtue that He has, since we can imagine nothing even in the gods better than prudence, justice, courage, and temperance. Therefore as God, through the possession of these virtues, is unconquered by pleasure or greed; is superior to desire, envy, and jealousy; is high-minded, beneficent, and kindly...so also humankind in the image [*mimema*] of Him, when living in accord with nature should be thought of as being like Him. (Frag. 17)

Paul does not believe in some abstract series of virtues or divine principles which are greater even than God and to which God and humankind ought to conform. For Paul, God in Christ is the very definition of virtue and true character. Second, since Paul believes human beings are fallen creatures, virtue is a matter of acting not according to nature or even one's own true nature, but according to grace and the promptings and guidance of the Holy Spirit in the life of a person who has become a new creature. As Galatians 5:16–26 suggests, virtue is a matter of living out the fruit of what the Spirit is producing in the believer's life by grace. Character formation is first and foremost a work of God in the believer. Believers must work out what God has worked in them and energized them to do. Lastly, note that even in 4:8 Paul does not extol the four cardinal virtues mentioned above in the passage from Musonius, which seem to have been a standard set since at least the time of Plato.[17]

Nevertheless, it is clear that in 4:8 Paul is drawing on concepts that did not come to him from early Christianity. Consider these four points: (1) two of the eight qualities mentioned in this list appear nowhere else in the NT (*prosphilē*, lovely;[18] *euphēma*, admirable); (2) one appears nowhere else in Paul (*aretē*); (3) one appears in the Pauline corpus only in the Pastorals (*semna*, noble); and (4) several have different senses here than elsewhere in Paul (*dikaia*).[19] The verse then deserves close attention.

We must first deal with a grammatical matter about the relationship between vv. 8–9. The *ha kai*, which connects vv. 8 and 9, has sometimes been taken as adversative, as if what is said in v. 9 must be taken almost as a corrective to what is said in v. 8.[20] The problem with this is that *kai* is hardly ever used as an adversative in the NT. We would expect *alla*.[21] Furthermore, in v. 9 there is a series of *kais*, not just one, which should all be translated the same way. Finally, the *ha* (which things) refers back to the virtues mentioned in v. 8, thus clearly linking the two verses. This, in turn, means that Paul previously taught the Philippians what is virtuous, noble, and the like. He is not leaving to their imagination the meaning and context for understanding these terms. Instead, he is clearly linking them to the gospel tradition earlier passed on to them and the example set for them by Paul himself and by Christ.

In v. 8 we again find the phrase *to loipon*. This might mean "finally," since Paul is drawing this section of the *peroratio* to a close,[22] but it is probable that here it means no more than "in addition."[23] These two verses are some of the most rhetorically powerful in the entire letter, including as they do a wide variety of literary devices.[24] Note that there are six two-word clauses in synonymous parallelism that are grammatically unconnected and thus emphatic, followed by two "if" clauses that summarize the preceding terms, followed by a series of injunctions connected by four *kais* (and) in v. 9, followed by a closing promise about God's peace. A Christian is urged to reflect on what is true, what is honorable[25] (or inspires reverence), whatever is right, whatever is pure, whatever is admirable, whatever is noble, if, as is the case, there is any virtue[26] or anything worthy of praise.

Aretē, without doubt, is the key word that was carried forward with some modifications into the Hellenistic and Roman periods and describes the moral ideal of the ancient Greeks. It refers not to any kind of excellence but to moral excellence or goodness. This had been a more general term in Greek for goodness of any kind, but in Stoic philosophy it had come to refer especially to human goodness, the end to which humans ought to devote themselves.

Paul says that Christians should ponder these things. The verb *logidzō* is a strong word meaning "to carefully take into account," "to calculate," and hence "to evaluate carefully a person or thing." It includes the idea of mulling things over and morally sifting them rather than making snap judgments. The main thing to be learned from v. 8 is that Paul is calling for Christians to be sifters, not rejecters, of their larger culture. He is suggesting that there are positive qualities to be seen in the world and believers should incorporate these into their Christian world view and way of living. He does not limit himself to Christian models of excellence but says that whatever is true and honorable (wherever one finds it) should be carefully examined and incorporated into one's walk if it is consistent with one's faith in and knowledge about Christ and his character. To be sure, one will use Christian standards to determine what is true and good, but when one finds it, it should be incorporated into the service of Christ.

Paul was not one who saw the church as all light and the world as all darkness. To the contrary, he believed the world was redeemable and occasionally manifested, by God's grace, redeeming qualities. Paul's vision of Christianity is that it is essentially a world-transforming, not a world-denying, religion, precisely because the world and all its creatures come from and belong to God, who has not given up on them.

One more thing should be noted concerning this catalog of virtues. Paul seems to believe that as one thinks, so one becomes. He also holds to the idea that one becomes like those one admires, hence the need for good moral exemplars, those who are worthy of praise. Yet he also thinks that there are human qualities one should appreciate wherever one finds them, even if found in a non-Christian. Thus, Paul urges the Philippians to focus on the good things.

Note that Paul is not content to urge his audience to sift the world for good examples. He closes this paragraph by urging that what the Philippians have received of church tradition and learned from the life of Paul they should put into practice, not least because this is the primary context in which they have seen modeled the Christian meaning and example of these virtues. The chief guide for behavior is the received Christian teaching about "these things," not what might be called general revelation.[27] Paul uses the word *parelabete,* a technical term used in early Judaism for the careful transmission and reception of sacred tradition (see 1 Cor. 15:3). Paul's letters intimate at points like Philippians 4:9 that Christianity did have a careful transmission of its own sacred traditions, including some of the sayings of Jesus.[28]

Paul and the Philippians — Partners, Friends, or Family?

There has been considerable debate by scholars in regard to what sort of relationship Paul had with the Philippians. Was it, as J. P. Sampley suggested, a sort of limited partnership, a *societas* relationship,[29] or was it a friendship with the usual set of Greco-Roman expectations brought into play,[30] especially in the hortatory sections of the letter? Or was it something different from both of these suggestions?

It is important to ask these questions in order to understand how Paul's parenesis functions in this relationship. Is it simply good advice from one friend to another of the same social and religious standing and status, or is some sort of hierarchical relationship implied by the letter such that Paul, while he would rather appeal, can give commands when necessary? Does Paul *appeal* to the Philippians because they are his equals or because he is engaging in rhetorical discourse that in the main requires persuasion and dissuasion rather than commands and demands?

Sampley's proposal has been critiqued by a variety of scholars including G. H. R. Horsley, L. Michael White, and especially G. Peterman.[31] The most serious flaws in his theory are as follows. First, Sampley has failed to demonstrate that *koinōnia* and its cognates are the normal equivalent of the Latin term *societas* and carry the latter term's legal connotations. The most natural Latin equivalent to *koinōnia* is surely *communis/communitas,* as Horsley points out.[32] Second, careful scrutiny of Paul's actual use of *koinōnia*, including in Philippians, does not suggest that he is using it as a legal or technical term in any case. It refers to common participation or sharing in something, which results in what we have come to call fellowship. Third, Sampley does not provide clear evidence of a *societas* relationship between an individual and a corporate or collective partner, which is what would be entailed if such a relationship existed between Paul and the Philippians. Fourth, as Peterman points out, when Paul addresses the issue of his right to support from his converts in 1 Corinthians 9, the reason he gives is not that he has a *societas* relationship with one or another group of his converts, but that he has a right to such support as an apostle.[33] Fifth, the phrase "to think the same thing" is not a technical one limited to the sphere of *societas* relationships. Though "*societas* demands being of the same mind, being of the same mind does not demand *societas*."[34] Sixth, White shows that the terminology to which Sampley points reflects a broader network of social relationships, including those of patronage, hospitality, and various sorts of friendships.[35]

What then should we make of White's attempt to connect Paul's language to Greco-Roman friendship conventions as a broader matrix for discussion? Certainly this proposal has more to commend it than Sampley's, for in fact the terms "friend" and "friendship" were used of a wide variety of relationships, including those between equals and those between a patron and a client.[36]

There are problems with this proposal, however. First, Paul eschews using the key term *philia* to describe his relationship with the Philippians.[37] White tries to circumvent this problem by following Malherbe's suggestion that Paul avoided the term because of its Epicurean associations. This is hardly convincing since the term *philia* and its cognates were used for a wide variety of relationships, and we have no reason to think there would be a particular Epicurean overtone read into the term by the Philippian converts. Second, White is too dependent on Sampley's reading of Philippians 4:10–20, where it is assumed that Paul, having solicited financial support from them, is calling on the Philippians to live up to their half of the friendship bargain, when in fact just the opposite is the case. Paul appreciates the gift but did not seek it or absolutely have to have it, as 4:17–18 make clear. Third, and most important, White basically ignores the very terminology that Paul does use to characterize the relationship he has with the Philippians, that is, the language of family. True brothers and sisters love each other and look out for each other, including financially, and this is the sort of healthy familial relationship Paul sees himself having with this and other groups of converts.

Yet there are also markers in the text that indicate that Paul does not see his relationship with the Philippians as one of absolute parity.

Although Paul here does not call himself their father in the faith, as he does elsewhere (e.g., 2 Cor. 12:14), it is clear enough from the appeal to imitation, from his sending Epaphroditus back, and from his promise to dispatch Timothy that there is some sort of hierarchical relationship still existing between Paul and these converts that cannot be described simply as friendship between equals.

The call to imitation is especially telling, as W. De Boer has recognized in his detailed study on Paul and imitation.[38]

> Paul's stance is like that of a father in the midst of the children he so dearly loved. Here too the matter of authority is not foreign to the relationship. . . . Paul here is the father who is seeking to lead, guide, direct and draw his children into the ways of his own life as a Christian. He is seeking the perfection of his own image as a Christian in them. . . . The processes here at work are more subtle than a direct urging of his authority and a pressing for obedience to his commands. . . . Paul's aim is to cultivate in his readers a living experience of the Christian way as he knows it. . . . The imitation of which Paul here speaks is not to be thought of as a mere . . . formal copying. . . . Paul is not worried that the Philippians might begin to take up a formal copying of the ways of the false teachers. The danger is that they will begin to *live* in that way. Paul counteracts by calling for imitation. . . . Paul's words here [in 4:9] indicate that Paul (as authorized teacher of Christianity) saw himself engaged in his teaching function not only in his formal acts of giving instruction, but also in the example he set in all of his life and conduct.[39]

Paul then is the mentor of the Philippians, and throughout this letter he is appealing, exhorting, and even at times directing (4:9) the Philippians as a teacher or a parent. I suspect that a pedagogical model of the relationship between Paul and the Philippians best explains the context in which the ethical advice in this letter should be read. There were many philosophical and rhetorical teachers in antiquity, and Paul seems to come across as a combination of the two. The pedagogical model for viewing this relationship is strongly supported by Paul's use of examples and the appeal to imitation *within a context of a rhetorical discourse.*

That Paul's relationship with the Philippians is friendly and affectionate, that in many respects he treats them as rather mature Christians and family, that he appeals for consensus in thought and behavior does not negate these conclusions. It simply shows that there is a good and warm relationship between the founder of the community and his converts. Paul does not need to trot out his credentials or to any degree pull rank on the Philippians, because he can rely on the art of persuasion and the general willingness of his audience to listen and respond to him.

The final line of the first part of this *peroratio* shows exactly what his relationship to these converts is (4:9). He is the one who has passed on the Christian tradition, told them the story of Christ, proclaimed the Good News to them, modeled the proper behavior and virtues for them, and he expects them to continue to practice the things that they have learned from him, which include continuing to imitate him. In short, Paul has not ceased to be their instructor in Christian living just because he is their friend and relative in the Lord. "Paul offers his own life as a screening room; those virtues which you have learned, received, heard, and seen in me, do these."[40]

Chapter Eleven _____

The *Peroratio* — 4:4–20

DIVISION II:
"GIVING AND RECEIVING" — 4:10–20

The last full discussion of any matter in this letter is found in the closing section of the *peroratio*. Keep in mind that the rhetorical function of such a section is to arouse strong positive feelings in the audience for the discourse just offered. Paul, wishing to further cement his strong ties with the Philippians, thanks them for their generous gift in an emotional passage laden with financial terminology.[1] Money, ever a delicate matter where Christian faith is concerned, was no less so for Paul. It was regular epistolary convention to write a personal note at the close of a letter, or at least to reserve very personal matters until then.[2] G. J. Bahr contends that the "thank-you note for the gift that Epaphroditus brought him was a highly personal matter for Paul, and so he wrote it in his own hand *at the end* of the subscription."[3] This is correct, and it is relevant to point out that there was no hard and fast line between letters and records or receipts in Paul's day. In other words, records and receipts often show up in the form of letters, or incorporated into letters, and Philippians 4:10–20 may provide an example of this practice.[4]

It is safe to say that Paul's financial dealings with his converts were complex, as even a casual reading of 1 and 2 Corinthians and Philippians will show. Let us first summarize how one should view this matter in general and leave the discussion of this particular passage until after the translation. It is fair to say that Paul is in part encouraged by the sending of the gift to him for:

...it did much more than help Paul defray expenses incurred. It testified to Paul that the gospel had taken root in the community, and consequently, that his mission had been successful. The Philippians' gift was a testimony to Paul that his work, in spite of the implicit risk of failure, is proving fruitful.[5]

In other words, at least in part, the Philippians were already modeling the sort of sacrificial, harmony-producing, Christ-like behavior to which Paul exhorts them in this letter.

Paul's Financial Dealings with His Converts

First of all, one should distinguish between what Paul says about the Collection and what he says about contributions of various sorts that were meant to benefit the Apostle himself and his own ministry. Paul did his best to avoid any sign of impropriety in regard to the Collection by delegating the handling of the matter to his own co-workers and those Christians appointed by local congregations to help gather, or at least deliver, the Collection (2 Cor. 8-9).[6] Our concern here is not with the Collection, which is nowhere mentioned in this letter, but with a relationship of "giving and receiving," which Paul says he had with no congregation other than the Philippians.

Paul is quite clear in 1 Corinthians 9 that he had both the right to receive and the right to refuse support from his converts while present with them, apparently on the basis of a teaching of Jesus about support of missionaries.[7] This does not tell the whole story, however.

I suggest that we distinguish types and degrees of financial support as follows. (1) Simple hospitality was the providing of bed and board when Paul was in a particular locale. This sort of practice seems in view in Romans 16:23, where Paul speaks of Gaius being Paul's host (*xenos mou*).[8] (2) Traveling funds were provided to a traveling missionary like Paul to "send him on his way," tiding him over until he arrived safely at his destination. We see this arrangement in 1 Corinthians 16:6b. (3) A relationship of ongoing "giving and receiving" would include missionary support to Paul from a congregation to aid him when he was working in another locale (Phil. 4:16). This plan required sending money to Paul to aid him personally when he was under house arrest (see Phil. 4:18ff.). Paul did not interpret this as a patron-client relationship but more of a parity relationship of some sort. Paul suggests that the Philippians' gift was reciprocity for what he had already given them. (4) Patronage, including ongoing in-house patronage, seems always to have been refused by Paul because it would place him in a position of being beholden to some Christian and make it difficult either for him to come and go freely as his missionary work required or to exercise his authority over all his converts in the location in question because he would be operating out of a position of social inferiority.

I suggest that Paul, both in the Corinthian correspondence and in 1 Thessalonians, is stressing that he has chosen to work in part to be able to turn down offers made of patronage. He says he does it so as not to be a burden on anyone (1 Thess. 2:9; 2 Cor. 12:13), or so as not to put an obstacle in the path of the reception of the gospel (1 Cor. 9:12).

Paul did not wish to become someone's in-house teacher or rhetor.[9] He did not charge fees like the Sophists, nor did he beg like some of the wandering Cynic preachers. It was a matter of principle for him that the initial proclamation of the gospel be offered free of charge, since the content of the message stressed grace, God's free gift in and of Christ. Since he rejected an ongoing patronage relationship that would have made him a client, this left him with options (1), (2), and (3) mentioned above, plus working, all of which he availed himself at various times.

It is clear that his financial relationship with the Philippians was distinctive: only they had the sort of agreement with him mentioned in (3) above, whereas even the Corinthians were allowed to help Paul in ways (1) and (2), despite all the problems in Corinth. It was in Paul's working and in his refusal of patronage and/or charging fees that he most stood out from other wandering preachers, teachers, and rhetors of his day. The persons of higher status among Paul's converts would likely have seen his manual labor as demeaning, and some apparently tried to relieve him of having to do it.[10]

Finally, it is worth pointing out that Paul's presence or absence in a situation affected how he responded to offers of financial support. Basically, Paul did not accept missionary support from a church *while* working with them in order to avoid any hint of impropriety, of offering the gospel for money, or of accepting patronage, all of which might hinder the cause.[11]

Translation

4:10 But I rejoiced in the Lord greatly because now at last your thought concerning me bloomed afresh, to whom you continue to give, but you lacked opportunity.[12] **11**I am not saying this because I lack anything, for I have learned how to be content/independent. [12]And I know what it is to be humbled and I know what it is to have an abundance. In all things and in everything I have learned the secret of how to be satisfied even if I am hungry, and I am able to go without. [13]I can cope with all these things in [union with] the one who strengthens me. [14]Nevertheless you do well to share in common my sufferings.

[15]But you yourselves know also, Philippians, that in the beginning of the gospel when I left from Macedonia not one church contributed to me for the settlement of giving and receiving except you alone, [16]because also in Thessalonica and more than once [elsewhere] you sent toward my need.[13] [17]Not that I search for the gift but I search for the strengthening of the interest for your account. [18]Here then is my receipt for everything: "Paid in full," receiving from Epaphroditus the things from you which have a sweet odor, an acceptable sacrifice pleasing to God. [19]But God will fully supply all your needs according to his riches in the glory in Christ Jesus. [20]But to God and our Father glory be unto aeons and aeons, Amen.

The specific matter discussed in 4:10–20 has been prepared for and alluded to at least three times earlier in the letter: in 1:4–5, 2:17, and 2:30.[14] This section, in particular 4:19–20, which provides the answers to Paul's intercessory prayer in 1:9–11, is related closely to the *exordium*.[15] That 4:10–20 is a self-contained subsection is shown by the now familiar introductory reference to joy in v. 10 and the concluding doxology in v. 20.[16] It also has an almost strophaic structure and rhythm, particularly in 4:11–13.[17] If Paul wrote this with his own hand, then it shows his compositional and rhetorical skills.[18]

This subsection relates to the overall strategy of the letter as follows. First, it reveals to the audience that indeed Paul believes they have been manifesting the sort of sacrificial Christian behavior that produces unity, a behavior encouraged in this letter; they were indeed, at least in part, living lives worthy of the gospel. Second, it reveals that the relationship of partnership in the gospel that the Philippians have with Paul, sharing each other's burdens, is a model of how the Philippians should be relating to each other. In other words, in this argument, the Philippians are shown to have already manifested a pattern of living that produces harmony, not discord, between persons.

Some scholars have been bewildered by what seems to be a damning of the Philippians with faint praise here, with the implication, "Don't send any more gifts" (remembering that Paul is even sending Epaphroditus back).[19] Silva suggests that a caricature of this passage might read as follows:

> I am glad that at long last, after waiting all this time, you finally decided to think about me. Of course, I realize you were meaning to do it — you just couldn't get around to it. I hope you understand, however, that I do not really need the money. My circumstances do not really bother me — I have learned how to handle all kinds of situations. Nevertheless, it's a good thing you decided to send the money — I mean for *your* sake, of course, not mine. You are really the ones that profit by sending an offering.[20]

This is indeed a caricature, not only because of the important parts of the argument that it leaves out, but also because it fails to read this argument in the light of the ancient reciprocity conventions.[21] Paul's attempt to make clear that he does not require such gifts is in part his way of reminding his listeners that he is not his audience's client and, even after receiving and accepting this gift, is not in their debt. Rather, he sees himself as the ambassador of their Benefactor, and what they have given is a matter of reciprocation. The one who initiated this relationship dictated its terms, as was common in such relationships. Paul had already set the tone and tenor of the relationship when he came to Macedonia.[22]

The relationship must be interpreted in light of the Philippians' ongoing debt to God in Christ, to whom Paul introduced his converts. They should look on their gift as a thanksgiving offering to God for what God had done through Paul in their lives, and it may also be that Paul "is viewing the gifts which he has received in terms of an investment by the Philippians upon which God will pay interest."[23]

It could be said, on the basis of a text like 2 Corinthians 11:8-9, that Paul was never fully comfortable accepting such gifts.[24] There he calls it robbery of the Macedonian churches, perhaps because he knew they were not wealthy; indeed some of the churches were impoverished (2 Cor. 8:2). Yet he *does* accept that he has a unique ongoing reciprocity relationship with the Philippians, a relationship of both giving and receiving, and he rejoices greatly that they have once again shown their concern for him. One should not minimize the significance of 4:10a and the thank you in 4:14,[25] but at the same time one must bear in mind that this response of Paul is both careful and complex. The letter as a whole leads one to affirm that "his words have to be read in light of the deep mutual affection existing between him and the Philippian church *and* in light of his well-attested financial policy."[26]

Paul is fully aware of the enmity conventions that would be set into motion if he refused their gift or simply returned it,[27] but this does not account for why he says he receives it very gladly. Notice that he interprets it as an offering to God, however, reminding the audience of to whom they are ultimately debtors. As for Paul himself, he says he has been paid in full for any and all services he had rendered to them; they owe him nothing. Their partnership in the gospel would continue, but the Philippians were not to think they *owed* Paul any more financial aid. It is difficult to convey to a modern audience how often in antiquity a gift had strings attached and normally placed the recipient in the giver's debt, requiring him or her to reciprocate in kind and even beyond in an ongoing cycle of oneupmanship.[28]

Regarding the exegesis of this passage, in v. 10 Paul turns to the delicate matter of the unsolicited gift he received from the Philippians. This is probably one of the major reasons for this letter, for Paul will go on to say that this letter is his receipt sent to the Philippians indicating he had been paid in full by them. The term *apechō* in v. 18 is the regular term marked on the bottom of a receipt meaning, "I have received in full." Paul approaches this subject cautiously, in part because he had a principle of not soliciting gifts of ministerial support but rather of providing for himself, accepting aid that had no strings attached or simply going without.

Yet this is not the first time the Philippians had sent him support. Verse 16 says that while Paul was in Thessalonica he received aid from the Philippians, and more than once elsewhere as well aid had arrived from them.[29] So Paul begins by saying that he rejoices abundantly that their concern has once again bloomed afresh for him. The verb *anethalete* refers to the springing into bloom of a bush or tree after a winter hiatus and does not suggest that their concern had ever died, only that circumstances were right to send help again only after a considerable interim. It is not clear why there had been such a long interim or why this gift came now. It may be that Paul's circumstances — perhaps his long journey to Rome and their lack of knowledge of his whereabouts — was a factor, or it may be that the Philippians themselves had only recently become able to send Paul money again.[30] We cannot tell with any certainty what had created the gap in giving.

Epaphroditus had been the deliverer of the gift, and now Paul was sending him back with the receipt as part of the letter he carried. Paul, however, makes clear to them as delicately as he can without sounding ungrateful that he did not absolutely have to have the gift. While the implied message may be "Don't send any more," Paul does not say so directly, for he does not wish in any way to put a damper on the Philippians' concern for Paul and his ministry or on their spirit of generosity.

In v. 11 Paul begins to explain his philosophy of the Christian life, which is in part to adjust to life's circumstances so that one is not dependent on variable factors for one's necessities or support. In a key phrase Paul says that he has learned how to be *autarkēs*. This term was common in Stoic and Cynic vocabulary to describe those who through discipline had become independent of external circumstances, discovering within themselves the necessary resources to cope with whatever the world threw at them. As Seneca once remarked, "The happy man is content with his present lot, no matter what it is, and is reconciled to his circumstances" (*De Vita Beata* 6).

Paul offers a significant variant to this philosophy, however, for he says in effect that the only independent person is the one who is dependent on the Lord for everything. Thus, he is preaching not a self-sufficiency, but a God-sufficiency.[31]

Paul knows how to enjoy abundance when it comes, but he also knows how to go hungry, how to do without, how "to be humbled," as he calls it. Though the use of this term is somewhat reminiscent of what Paul says about Christ in 2:8, there is a notable difference. Here Paul is not talking about conscious choices but of uncontrollable circumstances that humble a person, and the word is referring specifically to economic deprivation, not general affliction or spiritual abasement. The point is not that Paul had experienced such extremes of economic condition, but that he had learned during the course of his Christian life *how to live* in any and all circumstances.

In the memorable verse 13 Paul says, "I am able to face (or cope with) all these things in the One who strengthens me." Paul is not saying he is superhuman and can *do* anything. In context he is saying he has the inner strength or power to take whatever the world thrusts upon him. This is a very different matter. This verse is not a charter for thinking that one can accomplish anything if one draws on the strength of God. The context of coping with everything rather than seeking out or doing everything is also made clear in what follows in v. 14, where Paul adds, "nevertheless it is good of you to share in common with me in my sufferings." Paul presumably means that the Philippians have shared in his sufferings by helping to alleviate them.[32] Less likely is an allusion to the Philippians actually suffering for the Christian faith, although Paul has spoken of this fact elsewhere (see 2 Cor. 8:2; Phil. 1:29).[33]

In v. 15 Paul, as is his custom, uses the Roman designation for the residents of Philippi: the *Philippēsioi* (see Gal. 3:1; 2 Cor. 6:11).[34] Paul thus calls them by the Latinized form of the word, not the regular Greek form, a practice that would remind them of their Roman colonial status, in which no doubt they had pride since not every city was a Roman colony.[35] Yet it was a greater thing to have a commonwealth and Lord in heaven ruling them. Paul seems to use the vocative like this only when he is very vexed or very moved. I suspect this gift has moved or touched

Paul, even though he knows that accepting it could send mixed signals to other Christians where he was (see Phil. 1:15–18).[36]

The phrase "in the beginning of the gospel" (v. 15) is rather puzzling. Some commentators suggest that it means that Paul was in Philippi early in the 40s.[37] This requires that we dismiss not only the evidence of Acts, but also some of the hints in Paul's earlier letters, such as Galatians 1:18–2:1, that Paul ministered in Syria and Cilicia prior to ever coming to a place like Macedonia. It is unlikely that it means, "in the beginning of the preaching of the gospel [in Europe]," Philippi being the first port of call in Europe.[38] Nor is the suggestion that Paul considered all missionary work prior to Macedonia as preparatory or insignificant at all convincing.[39]

More likely we should place stock in the rest of v. 15a. What Paul says is, "in the beginning of the gospel when I *left* from Macedonia," so he probably means in the beginning of the missionary preaching that followed his time in Macedonia, which is supported by the interpretation suggested above of v. 16.[40] It is also supported by the similar phrase in 1:5, which suggests that Paul is talking about the point in time that the Philippians began to be his partners in the gospel.[41] In any case, the Philippians were the only ones who supported him when he was in Thessalonica and did so more than once after he left Macedonia.

Beginning in v. 15 Paul has chosen to use commercial metaphors concerning contributions, debits, and credits on an account. That the phrase *doseōs kai lēmpseōs* could and was used not only by pagans (see P. Teb. 2.277.16; Cicero *Lael.* 16.58, *ratio acceptorum et datorum*), but also by Jews to refer to debits and credits is clear from examining Sirach 41:19b and 42:7 ("When you make a deposit, be sure it is counted and weighed, and when you give or receive put it all in writing").

The question then becomes whether Paul is using the terms in a strict commercial sense or as a broader social metaphor to describe his relationship of reciprocity in regard to gifts and services with the Philippians, which of course included a financial component. Peterman shows that the broader sense is not only possible but well attested in more general discussions about "friendship" by Plutarch, Seneca, Epictetus, Cicero, and others, and I agree that Paul is using the phrase in the broader sense here.[42] This means that Paul is placing special stress on the financial aspect of such a relationship. But the phrase connotes a broader reciprocal relationship that includes the economic component. What taking the phrase in this broader sense would likely rule out is the suggestion that Paul saw this gift as a *payment* of a debt owed to him personally, one that arose out of some sort of preexisting contractual relationship that Paul had with the Philippians.[43]

Here a comment is in order concerning Sampley's contention that the word *chreia* in 2:25 (but also in 4:16, 19) refers not merely to Paul's need, but to the fact that he made a request for support from the Philippians.[44] This requires that we take this noun in the double sense of need-request, a rendering for which Sampley offers no evidence. Furthermore, this suggestion does not comport with what Paul plainly says in v. 17, that is, he does not (and did not) seek the gift![45]

Nonetheless, Paul in essence says that he is especially thankful for the gift, not because of what it does for him, but because it will be to the Philippians' credit, an enhancement of their heavenly account that God is keeping.[46] It should be added that, despite some disclaimers, Paul does believe in eternal rewards for Christian conduct. He does not see heaven as a reward, but there are rewards for good deeds when Christ returns (see 1 Cor. 3:14).[47] There is then a positive benefit for self as well as for others in doing good works, though Paul does not suggest this should ever be the motive for doing them.

In v. 18b Paul turns from a commercial to a sacrificial metaphor,[48] saying that their sacrifice had a pleasing odor to God, i.e., it was very acceptable in God's sight. Notice that v. 19 says that although they have made a sacrifice for the sake of the gospel, God will fully supply their every need according to his riches in glory.[49] This likely does not refer to heavenly rewards but to needs here and now. In other words, it is ultimately the case that the Philippians are in a relationship of giving and receiving with God in Christ, and they need to be clear about who is the true initiator and benefactor in this relationship. It is not the Philippians, or even Paul, but rather God who began a relationship with the Philippians through Paul.

Paul also seems to mean that God's supply comes to believers from where Christ is, in glory with God. From that storehouse in heaven he supplies the needs of God's people on earth, though of course he uses human beings to deliver the goods. It is important to stress that Paul does not say every wish or desire is granted if one relies on God, but that all needs are met. In Paul's view, this is the key to true independence from the world.

The sort of sacrifice Paul is discussing here is surely not a sin offering, but a thank offering in response to what God has already provided or done for the offerer.[50] The importance of this remark is that it shows that their gift was both accepted and acceptable. If it was pleasing to God, then surely Paul himself could not find it displeasing.[51] The implications of 4:19 are that in Paul's mind generous giving is an act of worship to God, indeed so much so that Paul speaks of their gift twice in this fashion (see 2:17 and 4:19).

It is also implied that the Philippians are acting as priests when they offer such gifts. It may be inferred that if Paul had been inclined to speak of priests in the Christian community, which he does not directly do, he would have spoken of the priesthood of all believers (see 1 Pet. 2:5, 9), or just possibly the high priesthood of Christ (see Hebrews), but not of a special class of clergy called priests who stand between God and God's people. Paul believes in the ministry of all Christians as an act of worship to God, though some are called to certain roles of leadership within the general ministry of the church.

Appropriately, after referring to the Philippians' giving as an act of worship, this section closes in v. 20 with a doxology, which again shows how grateful to God Paul is for the Philippians' generosity and sacrifice for the sake of the work of God. Such acts ultimately bring glory to God. It may be of some significance that Paul here, as in 1 Corinthians 15:24, stresses that God is "our Father." In a Roman colony it was the emperor who was given the important title "Father" in the form "Father of the fatherland."[52] Since colonies like Philippi and Corinth were treated as if they were on Italian soil, this title would have had special meaning to the Philippians. Paul then might be offering an alternative ideology for his converts: they should worship and give glory to the One who dwells in heaven, not to the "father" who dwells in Rome.[53] The letter's final argument closes with a pointer to the Ruler, commonwealth, and ruling principles that should guide these converts.

Chapter Twelve _____

Epistolary Closing/
Subscription – 4:21-23

"CAESAR'S HOUSEHOLD"

Translation

4:21Greet all saints in Christ Jesus. Those brothers with me greet you. 22All the saints greet you but most of all those from the household of Caesar. 23The grace of the Lord Jesus Christ be with your spirits.

There are no significant textual problems in this section.

As is true in other letters of Paul, the epistolary subscription is preceded by a closing doxology or benediction, in this case in 4:20 (cf. Rom. 15:33-16:1; 1 Thess. 5:23-26; 2 Thess. 3:16-17).[1] Traditionally in Greco-Roman letter writing, this section was devoted to final greetings and closing remarks. Unlike the normal pagan letter, which was apt to end with the stark "farewell" (*errosō/errosthe*) or occasionally "good luck" (*eutuxei*), Paul substitutes a closing benediction.[2]

Apart from the reference to Caesar's household, there is little that needs to be said about the closing greetings, although it is surprising that Paul never mentions anyone by name. This could be because there were divisions in Philippi and Paul did not wish to exacerbate them.[3] Yet there is a distinction made, for v. 21 is apparently addressed to the leaders mentioned in 1:1, who in turn are called upon to greet the rest of the saints there for Paul.

Return greetings from Christians who are with Paul are sent, and then we have the reference to the *Kaisaros oikias.*

A Closer Look: The Household of Caesar

The reference in Philippians 4:22 has led to a wide and even wild variety of speculations about the precise implications of Paul's use of *Kaisaros oikias.* It has even been assumed in older commentaries that Paul was indicating that some people of very high status had been converted to the faith.[4] This is not the case, if by higher status one has in mind patricians or other free members of Roman society. P. C. Weaver's detailed study of the numerous inscriptions about the *familia Caesaris* clearly shows that Paul is talking about slaves and freedmen in the service of the emperor and, in general, "an elite among the slave and freedman classes of Imperial society."[5] There was a clear social distinction between these imperial servants and freedmen and slaves outside the *familia Caesaris.* The elite members of the *familia Caesaris* were basically civil servants at the clerical and senior administrative levels, and some were even able to rise to auxiliary procuratorships, although they could never be the equal of the knight or equestrian procurators. At the lower end of the spectrum were those who had sub-clerical and, in some cases, even domestic roles. In general, members of the "household of Caesar" could be found in the provincial centers like Philippi or Corinth, but the largest single group was to be found in Rome itself, serving the emperor directly. In general, there were more opportunities, including opportunities for travel and advancement, for the imperial slaves and freedmen who served in Rome than for those who served in the provinces. Weaver stresses that the most mobile and most important, socially and professionally, of all the elements of the slave-born population of Rome were those who were part of the *familia Caesaris,* "especially among the holders of posts involving financial responsibility in the Imperial administration."[6] There were also the slave *dispensatores* in the "Household" who frequently traveled on errands for the emperor.

To judge from the sheer quantity of honorary inscriptions, it would appear that during the reigns of Claudius and Nero, the roles, status, and importance of the *familia Caesaris* reached new heights, but thereafter declined somewhat.[7] In other words, during the period when Paul visited the Philippians and then later wrote to them this group was an important part of Roman society, at the apex of its power and influence. Thus, on the one hand the greetings from Christians within this subset of society should be seen as greetings from some well-connected people, but on the other hand these Christians may be no more than slave couriers or part of the lower clerical, subclerical, or domestic orders of the *familia.*

It is plausible that the reason this group is greeting Philippians is that they know them, through travel on behalf of the emperor to his provincial center in Philippi. The social networks between Rome and the provincial centers were strong, and while not all roads led to Rome, it is more probable that this is a greeting sent from Rome to Philippi than, say, from Caesarea Maritima to Philippi, as the evidence of a close connection between those two centers is not forthcoming.[8] It is possible, of course, that this is a greeting from somewhere else, for instance, Ephesus, but we have no evidence of Paul being either under house arrest or in prison there. Of the over six hundred dated inscriptions that Weaver examined (not to mention a plethora of undated ones), the vast majority come from the *familia Caesaris* in Rome. I found only three from Ephesus, and two of these are almost certainly from the second century C.E.[9] Nevertheless, there is one famous inscription from Ephesus showing that the imperial freedmen and slaves there had formed themselves into a *collegia,* or club.[10]

To Lightfoot we owe the interesting conjecture that in Romans 16 we find the names of some of the Christian slaves and/or freedmen and freedwomen who were part of the *familia Caesaris* and sent greetings to the Philippians. Lightfoot bases this idea on the theory that Christianity first converted resident aliens and other non-Romans, including Jews in Rome, and that there were a significant number of such people in the imperial service.[11] This is all possible but unprovable. He is likely right, however, that these converts became Christians before Paul went to Rome.

●

A special greeting is sent from the household of Caesar — slaves and/or freedmen and women who have been converted from Caesar's wider entourage. This shows that the gospel was already working its way into high places, if only through the servant's entrance. This process would eventually culminate in the conversion of Constantine in about 300 C.E. In view of the fact that Paul distinguishes the group from Caesar's household from those Christians who are said to be with Paul in v. 21, it may be inferred that Paul is not being held where the household of Caesar could be found. This in turn may provide some confirmation for the view that the reference in Philippians 1:13 is not to the Praetorium, but to the Praetorian guard. In any case, the civil servants referred to in 4:22 should not be confused with soldiers keeping Paul under house arrest.[12]

One intriguing idea from Horsley is worth mentioning. There is clear evidence from as early as the time of Nero that there was an imperial monopoly on purple dye, its use and sale being monitored apparently by the emperor's civil service, which would involve the *familia Caesaris*. If this monopoly goes back to Claudius's time, then this raises the possibility that Lydia herself might be a member of the *familia Caesaris*.[13] If so, then the greetings in Philippians 4:22 could be from Lydia and her associates, now on business in Rome; however, we have no real way of knowing this to be the case. If Lydia was a freeborn woman rather than a freedwoman this conjecture becomes unlikely.

As always, Paul invokes upon his converts God's grace, which is to be with their spirits, Paul's normal term for their life. This is clearly a reference to their human life or spirit, and perhaps particularly to the spiritual side of their life, not a reference to the Holy Spirit in them.

Thus ends one of Paul's most eloquent and cordial letters, written to a group of generous converts who needed a deliberative appeal to rejoice and reflect in their attitudes and actions the Christ-like character and behavior that would produce concord and unity in their congregation. This would help them stand firm in the face of internal dissension and debates, and cope with possible external opponents who had and might again trouble this church.

Notes

Chapter One:
Background and Foreground of Paul
and the Philippian Letter

1. Some of what follows is found in a more detailed and modified form in my socio-rhetorical commentary on 1 and 2 Corinthians: *Conflict and Community in Corinth: A Socio-Rhetorical Commentary on 1 and 2 Corinthians* (Grand Rapids: Eerdmans, 1994).

2. Conclusions about some of these complex matters depend on how much stock one puts in the historical veracity of texts such as Acts 22:3-25. It is my working hypothesis that Luke has his facts straight at this point, whatever disputes there may be about other texts in Acts. The recent work of C. Hemer, *The Book of Acts in the Setting of Hellenistic History* (Winona Lake, Ind.: Eisenbrauns, 1989), 181-89, has once again shown that there is good reason to believe Luke is a rather reliable Hellenistic historian.

3. W. C. Van Unnik, *Tarsus or Jerusalem?* (London: Epworth, 1962), 8ff., points out that in Acts 22:3 *anatethrammenos* likely means "brought up" and in fact implies all his formative education took place in Jerusalem. He demonstrates that the three perfect-tense verbs in the sentence are often found together to refer to birth, early nurture, and education (see Plato *Alcib.* I.122B; Philo *de Leg. Alleg.* I.31 para. 99; Plutarch *Conv. disp.* 8 quest. 7 [727B]). Thus even what preschool education Paul had from his parents or relatives transpired in Jerusalem.

4. D. Daube, "Rabbinic Methods of Interpretation and Hellenistic Rhetoric," *Hebrew Union College Annual* 22 (1949): 239-62. Hillel's own teachers apparently first studied and taught in Alexandria, where, as Philo's work demonstrates, rhetoric was a main staple of all education and going to watch declaiming was a popular spectator sport (see Philo, *Worse Attacks the Better* 32-42). On the Greek of the rabbis, in the synagogue, and as part of a dialogue with Gentile synagogue adherents, see

S. Lieberman, *Greek in Jewish Palestine* (New York: Jewish Theological Seminary, 1942), 15ff.

5. E. A. Judge, "St. Paul and Classical Society," *Jahrbuch für Antike und Christentum* 15 (1972): 29.

6. See A. Segal, "The Cost of Proselytism and Conversion," *SBL 1988 Seminar Papers*, ed. D. J. Lull (Atlanta: Scholars Press, 1988), 336–69.

7. Strabo, *Geo.* 14.5.13–14, on rhetorical schools and the university in Tarsus surpassing Athens and Alexandria.

8. A. D. Nock's summary in *St. Paul* (London: Butterworth, 1938), 237, is reasonably apt: "The expression is externally Hellenic, but inwardly Jewish." Nock, however, while recognizing Paul's mastery of Greek with an "ear for rhythm" (27), his use of the diatribe style, and occasional rhetorical flourishes, thinks Paul did not use rhetoric and had "no social gospel" (180). This commentary seeks to show this judgment is wrong both about rhetoric and about Paul's social agenda. Nock is right, however, that the predominant influence on Paul's *thought* is not pagan philosophy but rather the OT and early Jewish and Christian traditions.

9. This is why a certain kind of reading of Acts can be misleading. Paul's missionary journeys were not merely evangelistic tours of various locations. In fact, it is questionable whether or not, after the first "missionary journey," the subsequent trips that Paul took should be called such. Journeys do not involve stopping in one place for a year and a half and practicing a trade, or in another for two or three years (on Ephesus, see Acts 19:10, 1 Cor. 16:8–9). I. H. Marshall, *Acts of the Apostles* (Leicester: Inter-Varsity, 1980), 214, reminds us: "Paul's missionary work[s] . . . [in] [t]he later periods were much more devoted to extended activity in significant key cities of the ancient world, and we gain a false picture of Paul's strategy if we think of him as rushing rapidly on missionary *journeys* from one place to the next, leaving small groups of half-taught converts behind him; it was his general policy to remain in one place until he had established the firm foundation of a Christian community, or until he was forced to move by circumstances beyond his control."

10. A. J. Malherbe, *Paul and the Popular Philosophers* (Minneapolis: Fortress, 1989).

11. Ibid., 76–77, emphasis mine. For a more detailed discussion of Paul's thought world see my *Paul's Narrative Thought World: The Tapestry of Triumph and Tragedy* (Louisville: Westminster/John Knox, 1994), and on Paul's indebtedness to Greek wisdom traditions see my *Conflict and Community.*

12. H. I. Marrou, *A History of Education in Antiquity* (New York: Sheed and Ward, 1956), 194–205.

13. See the discussion of R. A. Kaster, "Notes on 'Primary' and

'Secondary' Schools in Late Antiquity," *Transactions of the American Philological Association* 113 (1983): 323-46.

14. K. W. Niebuhr, *Heidenapostel aus Israel* (Tübingen: Mohr, 1992), 158ff.

15. Here I part company with D. Georgi and others. That Paul can and does deliberately distinguish himself from non-Christian Jews not only in Romans 9-11 but elsewhere in his letters and says he is capable of relating to either Jew or Gentile on virtually equal footing (see 1 Cor. 9) makes clear that he sees himself as a third sort of person, not just a Jew but a Jewish Christian. Fundamental to his thinking is that Jew and Gentile united in the Jewish Messiah Jesus are true Israel. In his view, non-Christian Jews are at least temporarily broken off from the covenant community until the full number of Gentiles are converted. Then, according to Romans 11, Paul expects a great turning of Jews to Christ, apparently through an eschatological miracle at the end of human history that will signal the return of Christ and the resurrection (see B. Witherington, *Jesus, Paul and the End of the World* [Downers Grove, Ill.: InterVarsity Press, 1992]). In short, Paul does not envision two different peoples of God co-existing at any point in human history. Thus, while it is true that Paul sees the Christian community as a development of early Judaism, one must also add that he believed that it was *the true or only proper* development of early Judaism. Paul was not an advocate of religious pluralism. See B. W. Winter, "Theological and Ethical Responses to Religious Pluralism — 1 Cor. 8-10," *Tyndale Bulletin* 41 (1990): 209-44.

16. On the subject of Paul's name one should compare T. J. Leary, "Paul's Improper Name," *New Testament Studies* 38 (1992): 467-69, and C. J. Hemer, "The Name of Paul," *Tyndale Bulletin* 36 (1986): 179-83. It is possible that *Paulos* was a nickname, "the small one," but more likely it was one of his three proper names, which a Roman citizen would have. We do not know what the other two were. According to Acts, Paul's name change does not occur at his Damascus road experience but when he begins to reach out to the Roman world, in this case to Sergius Paulus. Acts 13:9 introduces the change, saying Saul was also called Paul, which may in itself suggest a nickname. As Leary points out, once Paul became a missionary to the Gentiles there may have been an added reason not to call himself *Saulos*, as this word was used in Greek to describe the wanton style of walking of some prostitutes.

17. It is correct that this likely means most of the development in Paul's thought transpired *before* any of his letters were written.

18. The best brief introduction to Greco-Roman rhetoric is found in D. Watson, *Invention, Arrangement, and Style: Rhetorical Criticism of Jude and 2 Peter* (Atlanta: Scholars Press, 1988), 1-28. For more detailed treatments compare G. A. Kennedy, *New Testament Interpretation*

through Rhetorical Criticism (Chapel Hill: University of North Carolina Press, 1984), and B. Mack, *Rhetoric and the New Testament* (Minneapolis: Fortress, 1990).

19. C. Clifton Black II, "Rhetorical Criticism and the New Testament," *Proceedings of the Eastern Great Lakes* 8 (1988): 81.

20. Including insights from classics and Roman history scholarship.

21. The all too frequent evaluation that rhetoric was purely ornamental and made little real contribution to ancient culture in the Roman Empire is wrong. See, for example, P. Veyne, *A History of Private Life from Pagan Rome to Byzantium I* (Cambridge: Belknap, 1987), 22, who says rhetoric "most assuredly was not utilitarian; it contributed nothing to 'society.' "

22. See S. Benko, *Pagan Rome and the Early Christians* (Bloomington: Indiana University Press, 1984), 79ff.

23. Even the letter to Philemon has as a secondary audience, both the *ekklēsia* that meets in Philemon's house and his family.

24. It may be of some importance that Sophists were regularly hired as amanuenses in order to compose letters in proper rhetorical form. See A. Malherbe, *Ancient Epistolary Theorists* (Atlanta: Scholars Press, 1988), 3 and notes, and Philostratus *Lives* 590; 607. Could Paul have sometimes used a Christian scribe who was rhetorically trained? For example, when Paul stayed with Gaius in Corinth, while writing Romans (see 16:23) did he use Gaius's household scribe, named Tertius, who was rhetorically trained and also a convert? This might explain why some of Paul's letters do not seem to have much of a rhetorical form (see Colossians).

25. This may be why in Romans 16:1ff. Paul commends Phoebe and asks those in Rome to receive her and help her in all ways possible. See E. R. Richards, *The Role of the Secretary in the Letters of Paul* (Tübingen: Mohr, 1991), 190ff.

26. The phrase is borrowed from C. Roetzel, *The Letters of Paul: Conversations in Context,* 3d ed. (Louisville: Westminster/John Knox, 1991).

27. All of Paul's letters, except Romans and Colossians, are addressed to groups with whom he had a previous relationship.

28. W. J. Doty, *Letters in Primitive Christianity* (Philadelphia: Fortress, 1973), 26.

29. J. C. Beker, *Paul the Apostle: The Triumph of God in Life and Thought* (Philadelphia: Fortress, 1980), 351ff.

30. I owe this problem/progress distinction to my friend A. Chapple, "Local Leadership in the Pauline Churches: Theological and Social Factors in Its Development," D.Phil. diss., University of Durham, 1984, 1ff.

31. It is a fundamental principle of the interpretation of the Bible in general and these letters in particular that a document cannot

mean something today that would contradict the thrust or trajectory of meaning that was originally intended by the writer. It may well have larger significance or different applications today, but it ought not be applied in a way that violates the intended sense and meaning of the apostle. We must ask then what the text meant in its first-century context, and then in light of that ask what it might mean for us here and now. Only then will we be faithful to the text and be guided and guarded by its limits and allowances. It will be seen from this that I do not agree with various assumptions made by P. Ricoeur and some of the practitioners of reader-response criticism about the matter of intentionality and the *locus* of meaning. See B. Witherington, *Jesus the Sage: The Pilgrimage of Wisdom* (Minneapolis: Fortress, 1994), 150–55.

32. Rhetoric was a basic subject of ancient education throughout the Greco-Roman world. See S. F. Bonner, *Education in Ancient Rome: From the Elder Cato to the Younger Pliny* (Berkeley: University of California Press, 1977); D. L. Clark, *Rhetoric in Greco-Roman Education* (New York: Columbia University Press, 1957); M. L. Clarke, *Higher Education in the Ancient World* (London: Routledge and Kegan Paul, 1971). As A. D. Litfin, "St. Paul's Theology of Proclamation: An Investigation of 1 Corinthians 1–4 in Light of Greco-Roman Rhetoric," diss., Oxford, 1983, 202, says, "Rhetoric played a powerful and persuasive role in first-century Greco-Roman society. It was a commodity of which the vast majority of the population were either producers or, much more likely, consumers, and not seldom avid consumers." One did not have to be trained as a rhetor to appreciate hearing it or to develop a taste for it.

33. Later epistolary theorists stressed that letters should not take on a Sophistic or ornamental character, but should be written in a plainer, less elaborate style (e.g., avoiding long, rhetorically impressive periods and Atticism). On Philostratus of Lemnos, see Malherbe, *Ancient Epistolary Theorists,* 43. On the form, see F. X. J. Exler, *The Form of the Ancient Greek Letter* (Chicago: Ares, 1976), 23ff.

34. P. A. Meador, Jr., "Quintilian and the *Institutio oratoria,*" in J. J. Murphy, ed., *A Synoptic History of Classical Rhetoric* (Davis, Calif.: Hermagoras Press, 1983), 151. The rhetor was the one who dictated what would be taught in higher education.

35. For a detailed analysis of the formal characteristics of Pauline argumentation (such as the use of antithesis, typology, standing topics, aphorisms, analogies, arguments *a fortiori* and *ad hominem, ethos* and *pathos,* diatribe style, ellipsis, paradox, irony) that is rhetorically sensitive, see F. Siegert, *Argumentation bei Paulus gezeigt an Röm 9–11* (Tübingen: Mohr, 1985), 181–241.

36. See S. M. Pogoloff, *Logos and Sophia: The Rhetorical Situation of First Corinthians* (Atlanta: Scholars Press, 1992), 45ff. Some NT scholars

falsely assume that rhetoric has to do only with the form or style of a speech or letter.

37. T. Engsberg-Petersen, "The Gospel and Social Practice according to 1 Corinthians," *New Testament Studies* 36 (1990): 572-73.

38. The distinction between primary rhetoric, which deals with real subjects, and secondary rhetoric, or declamation, is an important one, especially since various first-century writers bemoan the decline of eloquence during the Empire. It was caused, they thought, by too much public declamation on esoteric topics, and also the rise of Asianism, a florid Eastern style of rhetoric. See G. A. Kennedy, *The Art of Rhetoric in the Roman World* (Princeton: Princeton University Press, 1972), 460, and Seneca *Ep.* 40.4, who says that the style of rhetoric of a philosopher should involve neither dragging out one's words, nor rushing headlong, for "speech which addresses itself, to the truth should be simple and unadorned." On opposition to declamation as an end in itself which flourished in the first century C.E., see Quintilian *Inst. Or.* 10.1.125-31.

39. G. A. Kennedy, *Classical Rhetoric: Its Christian and Secular Tradition from Ancient to Modern Times* (Chapel Hill: University of North Carolina Press, 1980), 68ff.

40. It will be seen from this conclusion that I am rejecting the older martyrological interpretation of Philippians of E. Lohmeyer and others. While suffering is a theme in this letter, it is not the focus of the argument. Basically Paul is not trying to teach his converts how to endure suffering or the rewards of doing so; he is trying to get his converts to all act and "think the same."

41. Kennedy, *Classical Rhetoric,* 74, on the insertion of epedeictic material in judicial or deliberative speeches to win the good will of the audience or discredit an opponent. See the judgment of D. E. Aune, *The New Testament in Its Literary Environment* (Philadelphia: Westminster, 1987), 203: "Most early Christian letters are multifunctional and have a 'mixed' character, combining elements from two or more epistolary types." I owe some of the following information to Janet Fairweather of the Classics faculty at Cambridge University.

42. Rhetoric was part of the training a well-to-do male went through in preparation for public office, whether he was to be an aedile or a proconsul, or simply a legal advocate or ambassador. This may be of some importance in discerning who was complaining in Corinth about Paul's rhetoric, or lack of rhetorical polish (namely, well-to-do Gentile males).

43. Cicero, *Pro Marcello.*

44. Malherbe, *Ancient Epistolary Theorists,* 66-67. The last type mentioned is *mixte.*

45. See Chrysostom's commentary on Galatians on 6:18. On mixed rhetoric, see also Dionysius of Halicarnassus, vol. 6., *Opuscula II,* ed. H. Usener and L. Radermacher (Leipzig: Teubner, 1933), the treatise

"peri eschematismenon." One may also wish to consider Demosthenes' famous *De Corona* speech. See also L. G. Bloomquist, *The Function of Suffering in Philippians* (Sheffield: JSOT Press, 1993), 84ff., on the mixed rhetorical letter type.

46. The reader wishing a basic introduction to rhetoric by a first-century practitioner of the art, who sums up many of the developments that came before him, should read Quintilian, *Institutio Oratoria*, Books 4-10, most conveniently found in the Loeb Classical Library, trans. H. E. Butler (Cambridge: Harvard University Press, 1966 rpr.)

47. Marrou, *History of Education*, 196-97.

48. Ancient writers did distinguish between the average letter and a speech (see Aristotle, *Rhetoric* 3.12.1; Pliny *Letters* 5.8; Demetrius, *On Style*, 223.25-28), but Quintilian lets us know that letters that were in effect meant for proclamation, and thus to a large extent written versions of a speech, were closer to a speech than to an ordinary letter in character (*Inst. Or.* 12.10.53-55). Paul has blended the letter and speech conventions, so that apart from the epistolary opening and closing of the letter one can evaluate the letter in terms of the rhetorical conventions. In short, the thanksgiving section and the body of the letter can be evaluated this way.

49. Marrou, *History of Education*, 195.

50. Aune, *New Testament*, 12-13.

51. Marrou, *History of Education*, 204-5.

52. Consider the papyrus fragment dating to about 110 C.E., which reads in part: "Pay to Licinnius...the rhetor the amount due him for the speeches [in] which Aur[elius...] was honored...in the gymnasium in the Great Serapeion, four hundred drachmas of silver." See R. K. Sherk, *The Roman Empire* (Cambridge: Cambridge University Press, 1988), 195. This was more than what a Roman soldier would be paid for an entire year's service, according to Tacitus *Annals* 1.17.

53. During the Empire assemblies were allowed less and less legislative freedom and often were reduced to merely electing magistrates. This may explain another reason why those who valued freedom were looking for another *ekklēsia* where debate and dialogue would still be carried on. The very term *ekklēsia* would have suggested to some that the Christian meeting was the place for such debates and the use of rhetoric, particularly deliberative rhetoric.

54. See Pogoloff, *Logos and Sophia*, 62: "In the Imperial period, rhetoric was particularly open to attack. Since opportunities for meaningful public address were greatly curtailed, rhetorical display was often reduced to showpieces, and Stoic philosophers claimed it had lost its content and become empty playing with style."

55. While there are a few isolated examples in the literature of women, such as Hortensia, the daughter of the famous rhetor Q. Hort-

ensius Hortalus, delivering an oration, in this case to the triumvirs in 42 B.C.E., I know of no examples of women who were regularly practicing or professional rhetors. Hortensia no doubt gained her skills in the home, for it was not the normal practice for women to have "higher education," which means that even well-to-do women lacked training in rhetoric beyond the progymnasta level. See E. Cantarella, *Pandora's Daughters* (Baltimore: Johns Hopkins University Press, 1987), 141 and 214, n. 12, and Quintilian *Inst. Or.* 1.1.6.

56. On its history and development during the Empire, see S. F. Bonner, *Roman Declamation in the Late Republic and Early Empire* (Liverpool: Liverpool University Press, 1949), 26ff. The basic meaning of declamation in antiquity was "the consideration of a subject without any reference to specific circumstances." On this showing this is just the opposite of Paul's sort of rhetoric.

57. I am indebted to my friend and colleague Dr. Duane F. Watson not only for our numerous conversations in the past year about rhetoric, which helped me articulate my thoughts about Philippians, but also for his fine article, "A Rhetorical Analysis of Philippians and Its Implications for the Unity Question," *Novum Testamentum* 30 (1988): 57–87. It will be seen that I disagree with him in some particulars about the rhetorical arrangement, while strongly agreeing with his judgment that the letter can be seen as a rhetorical unity. See his more detailed and technical commentary on Philippians forthcoming from Eerdmans.

58. Paul uses a similar rhetorical strategy in Philemon, where it does not appear until the letter is almost over what Paul is really asking of Philemon, namely, that he free Onesimus and send him back to Paul to assist the apostle.

59. The full rhetorical analysis of Philippians by Bloomquist, *Function of Suffering,* 119ff. should be considered. I agree with him in the delineation of the *exordium,* but he mistakes 1:15–18a for the *propositio,* when it does not come until 1:27–30, as D. Watson has shown. He also makes the mistake of including 3:17–4:7 as part of one final argument, an *exhortatio,* when in fact this section includes several discrete units of material with different rhetorical functions. There is, nonetheless, much to be gained from his analysis of how individual arguments function.

60. J. Weiss, *Beiträge zur Paulinischen Rhetorik* (Göttingen: Vandenhoeck & Ruprecht, 1897). Weiss especially stresses the artful form of Philippians 1:13–17 (17ff.) and of 4:11–13 (29) in the second portion of the *peroratio.*

61. See Hemer, *Book of Acts,* 393.

62. This does not mean there was not a regular Jewish meeting outside the city walls, as the text may suggest, since the term *proseuchē* was the standard term for a Jewish meeting place in the Diaspora.

63. B. Witherington, *Women in the Earliest Churches* (Cambridge: Cambridge University Press, 1988), 111–13 and notes.

64. Ibid., 12–14; W. W. Tarn and G. T. Griffith, *Hellenistic Civilisation,* 3d ed. (London: E. Arnold, 1952), 98ff.; S. Pomeroy, *Goddesses, Whores, Wives, and Slaves* (London: R. Hale, 1975), 120ff.

65. R. MacMullen, "Woman in Public in the Roman Empire," *Historia* 29 (1980): 208–18, here 214. The conjecture she was only the wife of a high priest seems a less plausible reading of the inscription.

66. See L. Michael White, "Morality Between Two Worlds; A Paradigm of Friendship in Philippians," in D. L. Balch et al., eds., *Greeks, Romans, and Christians* (Minneapolis: Fortress, 1990), 206.

67. See G. Hawthorne, *Philippians* (Waco, Tex.: Word, 1983), xxxv. We may mention Epaphroditus, Euodia, Syntyche and Clement.

68. On the historical substance of this account see Witherington, *Women in the Earliest Churches,* 147–49.

69. A helpful collection of preliminary essays on this matter can be found in L. Michael White, ed., *Social Networks in the Early Christian Environment: Issues and Methods for Social History,* Semeia 56 (Atlanta: Scholars Press, 1992).

70. On this see the commentary on Philippians 4:22 and the excursus there on p. 135.

71. G. W. Peterman, "Giving and Receiving in Paul's Epistles: Greco-Roman Social Conventions in Philippians and Other Pauline Writings," Ph.D. diss., King's College, University of London, 1992, forthcoming in the Society for New Testament Studies monograph series from Cambridge University Press.

72. J. Paul Sampley, *Pauline Partnership in Christ* (Philadelphia: Fortress, 1980).

73. On the subject of patronage in the Roman Empire in general see Witherington, *Conflict and Community in Corinth,* and R. P. Saller, *Personal Patronage under the Empire* (Cambridge: Cambridge University Press, 1982).

74. See A. H. M. Jones, "Imperial and Senatorial Jurisdiction in the Early Principate," *Historia* 3 (1955): 464–88 and G. P. Burton, "Proconsuls, Assizes and the Administration of Justice under the Empire," *Journal of Roman Studies* 65 (1975): 92–106. It is clear enough that by Paul's day the appeal to Caesar over the head of the provincial officials was possible. Such a practice was already possible during the reign of Augustus.

75. See D. Georgi, *Remembering the Poor* (Nashville: Abingdon, 1992), 63ff. and notes. This conjecture in part depends on the further conjecture that 4:10–23 is a letter fragment. See p. 125 below on the actual character of this subsection and on its important role as part of the rhetorical unity of the letter.

76. See M. Silva, *Philippians* (Grand Rapids: Baker, 1992), 6–7 and notes.

77. For what it is worth, the second-century Marcionite prologue connects this letter with a Roman imprisonment.

78. W. J. Dalton, "The Integrity of Philippians," *Biblica* 60 (1979): 97–102; S. E. Fowl, *The Story of Christ in the Ethics of Paul* (Sheffield: JSOT Press, 1990), 49ff.

79. Watson, "Rhetorical Analysis," 83.

80. R. Jewett, "The Epistolary Thanksgiving and the Integrity of Philippians," *Novum Testamentum* 12 (1970): 40–53; D. Garland, "Philippians 1:1–26: The Defense and Confirmation of the Gospel," *Review and Expositor* 77 (1980): 327–36; and his "The Composition and Unity of Philippians," *Novum Testamentum* 27 (1985): 141–71.

81. G. Lyons, *Pauline Autobiography: Toward a New Understanding* (Atlanta: Scholars Press, 1985); J. L. Sumney, *Identifying Paul's Opponents: The Question of Method in 2 Corinthians* (Sheffield: JSOT Press, 1990).

82. So Watson, "Rhetorical Analysis," 80ff.

83. See the discussion in G. D. Kilpatrick, "*Blepete,* Philippians 3:2," in M. Black and G. Fohrer, eds., *In Memoriam, Paul Kahle* (Berlin: Töpelmann, 1968), 146–48.

Chapter Two:
Epistolary Prescript — 1:1–2

1. P. T. O'Brien, *Commentary on Philippians* (Grand Rapids: Eerdmans, 1991), 44.

2. See L. G. Bloomquist, *The Function of Suffering in Philippians* (Sheffield: JSOT Press, 1993), 140ff.

3. See B. Mengel, *Studien zum Philipperbrief* (Tübingen: Mohr, 1982), 223–24.

4. V. Parkin, "Some Comments on Pauline Prescripts," *Irish Biblical Studies* 8 (1986): 92–99, suggests that Paul mentions his apostolic status in prescripts when his authority is being challenged by the audience he is about to address. Paul calls himself *doulos* in a prescript only here and in Romans 1:1, and elsewhere at 2 Corinthians 4:5 and Galatians 1:10. It must have some particular function in this discourse, and the most persuasive suggestion is that Paul is setting an example of proper leadership.

5. See D. Garland, "Philippians 1:1–26: The Defense and Confirmation of the Gospel," *Review and Expositor* 77 (1980): 327–28.

6. Bloomquist, *Function of Suffering,* 140ff.

7. Ibid., 148ff., rightly sees this point.

8. See my extended discussion of the way Greco-Roman meals proceeded and how this affected the church in Corinth in *Conflict*

and Community in Corinth: A Socio-Rhetorical Commentary on 1 and 2 Corinthians (Grand Rapids: Eerdmans, 1994), 191–95.

9. B. Holmberg, *Paul and Power* (Philadelphia: Fortress, 1978), 116.

10. It is interesting that, with the exception of Philemon, it is only in letters to the Macedonian congregations (Philippi and Thessalonica) that Paul fails to mention his apostolic status at the beginning of a letter. Perhaps this is because they were some of his least troubled congregations, so far as the issue of the authority structure was concerned. See M. Silva, *Philippians* (Grand Rapids: Baker, 1992), 39.

11. See W. A. Meeks, *The First Urban Christians* (New Haven: Yale University Press, 1983), 133ff.

12. For a helpful graph of the link Timothy provides for Paul to various of his congregations when he is away from them (Corinth, Thessalonica, Philippi, Colossae, and perhaps Ephesus), see R. A. Atkins, *Egalitarian Community: Ethnography and Exegesis* (Tuscaloosa: University of Alabama Press, 1991), 106–7.

13. G. Hawthorne, *Philippians* (Waco, Tex.: Word, 1983), 11.

Chapter Three:
Exordium and Thanksgiving Prayer — 1:3–11

1. This list is partly adopted from D. F. Watson, "A Rhetorical Analysis of Philippians and Its Implications for the Unity Question," *Novum Testamentum* 30 (1988): 64.

2. J. B. Lightfoot, *St. Paul's Epistle to the Philippians* (London: Macmillan, 1894), 83.

3. Watson, "Rhetorical Analysis of Philippians," 62.

4. See J. Y. Campbell, "*Koinonia* and Its Cognates in the NT," *Journal of Biblical Literature* 51 (1932): 352–80; H. Seesemann, *Der Begriff Koinonia im Neuen Testament* (Giessen: Töpelmann, 1933).

5. G. W. Peterman, "Giving and Receiving in Paul's Epistles: Greco-Roman Social Conventions in Philippians and Other Pauline Writings," Ph.D. diss., King's College, University of London, 1992, 107ff., forthcoming in the Society for New Testament Studies monograph series from Cambridge University Press.

6. The grammar of v. 3a permits either rendering; see M. Silva, *Philippians* (Grand Rapids: Baker, 1992), 44ff.

7. See G. Hawthorne, *Philippians* (Waco, Tex.: Word, 1983), 24. *Apologia* and *Bebaiosis* were technical legal terms used in the law courts of the Empire to refer to defense and vindication of a particular cause or case.

8. See A. N. Sherwin-White, *Roman Society and Roman Law in the New Testament* (Grand Rapids: Baker, 1963), 20ff.; and compare my discussion of 1 Corinthians 6 in *Conflict and Community in Corinth:*

A Socio-Rhetorical Commentary on 1 and 2 Corinthians (Grand Rapids: Eerdmans, 1994), 162–69.

9. Sherwin-White, *Roman Society,* 111.

10. Ibid., 108–9.

11. Hawthorne, *Philippians,* 25.

12. Silva, *Philippians,* 57–58. This is surely another point in favor of the view that Philippians is likely one of the later Pauline letters, written about the same time as Colossians.

13. J. Weiss, *Beiträge zur Paulinischen Rhetorik* (Göttingen: Vandenhoeck & Ruprecht, 1897), 9ff.

14. R. Jewett, "The Epistolary Thanksgiving and the Integrity of Philippians," *Novum Testamentum* 12 (1970): 51–52. He also demonstrates the numerous other substantive terminological connections that link all four chapters together (52ff.).

Chapter Four:
The *Narratio* — 1:12–26

1. See D. Garland, "Philippians 1:1–26: The Defense and Confirmation of the Gospel," *Review and Expositor* 77 (1980): 331: "The 'rather' ... of verse 12 implies that they had expected the worse, and they were obviously concerned or they would not have taken it upon themselves to dispatch Epaphroditus with a gift."

2. See Quintilian *Inst. Or.* 3.8.11: "Statements [in deliberative discourses] as to external matters which are relevant to the discussion may however be frequently introduced."

3. M. M. Mitchell, *The Rhetoric of Reconciliation* (Tübingen: Mohr, 1991), 200–201.

4. See Garland, "Defense and Confirmation" 331.

5. See J. Weiss, *Beiträge zur Paulinischen Rhetorik* (Göttingen: Vandenhoeck & Ruprecht, 1897), 17.

6. See Lightfoot's extended note on this in *St. Paul's Epistle to the Philippians* (London: Macmillan, 1894), 101–4. For a case similar to Paul's of a Jewish person under house arrest in Rome, chained to a soldier and in the care of the Praetorian guard, see Josephus *Ant.* 18.6.5ff.

7. See F. F. Bruce, *Philippians* (New York: Harper & Row, 1983), xxii. The inscriptional evidence (see *Corpus inscriptionum latinarum* III. 6085, 7135, 7136) for a *praetorianus,* a Praetorian guard in the region of Ephesus, is irrelevant for, as Bruce points out, this person is a *former* Praetorian guard, now only a *stationarius* or policeman on a Roman road near Ephesus.

8. See F. Craddock, *Philippians* (Atlanta: John Knox, 1985), 26: "These divisive preachers are not the famed Judaizers of Corinth, Gala-

tia, and perhaps chapter 3 of Philippians. They cannot be. The Judaizers preached another gospel and for it received Paul's anathema (Gal. 1:6–9). Even a dying Paul would rise on one elbow to fight with them. Here the issue is not message but motive."

9. So D. F. Watson, "A Rhetorical Analysis of Philippians and Its Implications for the Unity Question," *Novum Testamentum* 30 (1988): 63ff.

10. See M. Silva, *Philippians* (Grand Rapids: Baker, 1992), 77.

11. Ibid., 76–78.

12. G. Hawthorne, *Philippians* (Waco, Tex.: Word, 1983), 44–45.

13. See the discussion in B. Witherington, *Jesus, Paul and the End of the World* (Downers Grove, Ill.: InterVarsity Press, 1992), 203ff.

14. Craddock, *Philippians*, 28–29.

15. See the helpful discussion in D. B. Martin, *Slavery as Salvation: The Metaphor of Slavery in Pauline Christianity* (New Haven: Yale University Press, 1990), 48ff.

16. H. Moxnes, "Honor, Shame, and the Outside World in Paul's Letter to the Romans," in J. Neusner et al., eds., *The Social World of Formative Christianity and Judaism* (Philadelphia: Fortress Press, 1988), 213.

17. Witherington, *Conflict and Community*, 154–55. See the whole excursus on honor and shame there.

18. See Silva, *Philippians*, 66ff.

Chapter Five:
The *Propositio* — 1:27–30

1. See M. M. Mitchell, *The Rhetoric of Reconciliation* (Tübingen: Mohr, 1991), 198.

2. Roman colonies cities differed in certain key respects from other cities in the Empire: (1) their form of government was the same as Roman towns in Italy, and their laws were Roman laws; (2) the vast majority of the ruling strata of society in a colony was made up of former Roman soldiers, Italian citizens, and Roman freedmen; (3) if the city was a new one, or even if it was not, its design would be set up or modified to suit a Roman plan; (4) Greek natives of the city became *incolae*, or non-citizens, for the most part, since Roman citizenship was the sort that really counted in such a place. See my discussion in *Conflict and Community in Corinth: A Socio-Rhetorical Commentary on 1 and 2 Corinthians* (Grand Rapids: Eerdmans, 1994), 5ff.

3. Pace R. E. Brewer, "The Meaning of *Polistheusthe* in Phil. 1:27," *Journal of Biblical Literature* 73 (1954): 76–83.

4. The attempt to read Paul's use of *politeusthe* in light of the use in the Intertestamental literature by E. C. Miller, "*Politeusthe* in Philippians 1:27: Some Philological and Thematic Observations," *Journal for*

the Study of the New Testament 15 (1982): 86-96, is not fully convincing as M. Silva, *Philippians* (Grand Rapids: Baker, 1992), 90, n. 1, shows.

5. See B. Witherington, *Jesus, Paul and the End of the World* (Downers Grove, Ill.: InterVarsity Press, 1992), 184ff.

6. *Psuchē* can refer to physical life or physical life breath; see 1 Corinthians 15:45, 1 Thessalonians 5:23. It does not mean "soul" in Paul, i.e., the non-material part of the person. For this Paul uses the term *pneuma*. See Witherington, *Jesus, Paul and the End of the World*, 198ff.

7. J. B. Lightfoot, *St. Paul's Epistle to the Philippians* (London: Macmillan, 1894), 27.

8. Silva, *Philippians*, 95. The dative of advantage may be in evidence here, if one compares the similar construction in 2 Timothy 1:8 and 3 John 8. See D. R. Hall, "Fellow Workers with the Gospel," *Expository Times* 85 (1974): 119-20. But if so, what would striving along with the faith of the gospel mean, especially since the dative of advantage normally requires a person who gains the advantage referred to?

9. G. Hawthorne, "The Interpretation and Translation of Philippians 1:28b," *Expository Times* 95 (1983-84): 80-81. See the critique by P. T. O'Brien, *Commentary on Philippians* (Grand Rapids: Eerdmans, 1991), 154-55.

10. In an important lecture, "Paul the Controversialist," given at Ashland Seminary in 1990, C. K. Barrett suggested that the Judaizers were actually seeking Paul's death, seeing him and his message as a serious threat to their whole religious way of living (see 2 Cor. 12:26: "dangers from false brothers"). If this is the case, it would not be surprising if they also tried pressure and perhaps even persecution of some sort against some of Paul's more loyal converts as well. This would explain the polemics in chapter 3, referring to the adversaries as those who "live as enemies of the cross of Christ." In Paul's view, to live as the Judaizers were doing was possible only if one was ignorant of, ignored, or repudiated the view that Christ's death had set believers free from the obligation to keep the law of Moses.

11. V. C. Pfitzner, *Paul and the Agon Motif: Traditional Athletic Imagery in the Pauline Literature* (Leiden: Brill, 1967), 76ff.

12. G. Caird, *Paul's Letters from Prison* (Oxford: Oxford University Press, 1976), 115.

13. For more on this see B. Witherington, *Paul's Narrative Thought World: The Tapestry of Triumph and Tragedy* (Louisville: Westminster/ John Knox, 1994), part 3.

14. J. H. Schütz, *Paul and Apostolic Authority* (Cambridge: Cambridge University Press, 1975), 50.

Chapter Six:
The *Probatio* — 2:1–4:3:
The First Appeal — 2:1–18

1. J. Weiss, *Beiträge zur Paulinischen Rhetorik* (Göttingen: Vandenhoeck & Ruprecht, 1897), 28, stresses the parallel grouping, dividing the hymn into two four-part strophes.

2. B. Witherington, *Conflict and Community: A Socio-Rhetorical Commentary on 1 and 2 Corinthians* (Grand Rapids: Eerdmans, 1994).

3. See D. Garland, "Philippians 1:1–26: The Defense and Confirmation of the Gospel," *Review and Expositor* 77 (1980): 172.

4. F. Stagg, "Philippians" in *Broadman Bible Commentaries* (Nashville: Broadman Press, 1971), 11:183, 202.

5. See D. Garland, "The Composition and Unity of Philippians," *Novum Testamentum* 27 (1985): 172.

6. L. G. Bloomquist, *The Function of Suffering in Philippians* (Sheffield: JSOT Press, 1993), 191ff., attempts to see Paul as the *causa* in and of this discourse; this is hardly convincing. Paul is to be seen as but one example among several, the primary being Christ.

7. B. Witherington, *Paul's Narrative Thought World: The Tapestry of Triumph and Tragedy* (Louisville: Westminster/John Knox, 1994), chap. 3, and the important work by S. E. Fowl, *The Story of Christ in the Ethics of Paul* (Sheffield: JSOT Press, 1990), 49ff., for his lengthy discussion of Philippians 2:6ff., demonstrating how it functions to provide an example for Paul's audience.

8. D. A. Black, "Paul and Christian Unity: A Formal Analysis of Philippians," *Journal of the Evangelical Theological Society* 28, no. 3 (1985): 299–308.

9. Chiasm is a literary device where the first and last elements of a literary unit are either identical or nearly so. The basic form is A, B, A, or as in the case of this text A, B, B, A, where there are two middle elements offering two different ways to speak of the same second subject.

10. Bloomquist, *Function of Suffering*, 165ff.

11. It is a major mistake to see the appeal to Christ's example as a way of explaining the more primary example in this letter of Paul himself, as Bloomquist, *Function of Suffering*, 168–69, does.

12. See F. Craddock, *Philippians* (Atlanta: John Knox, 1985), 35: "Paul is not raising any question or doubt about the quality or genuineness of the Philippians' faith and life. On the contrary he is not only affirming them but is building his call for progress and maturity upon those very faith and life experiences."

13. On the goal of this material being to produce unity in the Chris-

tian community, as is clear from the use of "mind" in vv. 1–2, 5, see B. Mengel, *Studien zum Philipperbrief* (Tübingen: Mohr, 1982), 243.

14. E. Lohmeyer, *Der Brief an die Philipper, an die Kolosser und an Philemon* (Göttingen: Vandenhoeck & Ruprecht, 1956), 82.

15. W. Barclay, "Great Themes of the New Testament: I. Phil. 2:1–11," *Expository Times* 70 (1958–59): 5.

16. Rightly Barclay, "Great Themes," 6.

17. J. B. Lightfoot, *St. Paul's Epistle to the Philippians* (London: Macmillan, 1894), 108–9.

18. See the discussion of Paul's use of these terms, which were common political terms used in deliberative rhetoric, in M. M. Mitchell, *The Rhetoric of Reconciliation* (Tübingen: Mohr, 1991), 68ff.

19. See my discussion of the more serious problems of this nature in Corinth in Witherington, *Conflict and Community.*

20. On Paul's indebtedness to the Wisdom tradition, see B. Witherington, *Jesus the Sage* (Minneapolis: Fortress, 1994).

21. On these allusions to Isaiah 52–53 see Bloomquist, *Function of Suffering*, 162ff. It is a mistake to read this hymn, as Bloomquist does, as a story of Christ submitting to inescapable suffering, just as Paul is thought to be doing. This hymn is about attitude and action and making the right choices. Surely the point is that the Son chose to humble himself not merely in the act of suffering and dying, but in the very act of taking on human form. In other words, humbling has to do with taking on a lower social status and station for the good of others, not with abandonment or fruitlessness per se (contrast Bloomquist, *Function of Suffering*, 164).

22. O. Merk, *Handeln aus Glauben: Die Motivierungen der paulinischen Ethik* (Marburg, 1968), 177ff.

23. On social status in the Roman world and its importance, see Witherington, *Conflict and Community*, 259–60, and also P. Garnsey, *Social Status and Legal Privilege in the Roman Empire* (Oxford: Clarendon, 1970), 221ff.

24. G. Hawthorne, *Philippians* (Waco, Tex.: Word, 1983), 79ff.

25. See I. H. Marshall, *Philippians* (London: Epworth, 1991), 48: "*Among yourselves* indicates that Paul is thinking of their attitudes towards one another that come to expression in how they treat each other."

26. But see the counterarguments in M. Silva, *Philippians* (Grand Rapids: Baker, 1992), 108ff. He is right, however, that the translation "among you" rather than "within you" is to be preferred. For the latter we would have expected *heautois.*

27. Pace Barclay, "Great Themes," 41.

28. E. Käsemann, "A Critical Analysis of Philippians 2:5–11," *Journal for Theology and the Church* 5 (1968): 45–88.

29. Stagg, "Mind of Christ," 342.

30. See the discussion of S. E. Fowl, *Story of Christ in the Ethics of Paul,* 88ff., and Witherington, *Paul's Narrative Thought World.*

31. See the discussion in R. MacMullen, *Roman Social Relations 50 B.C.E. to A.D. 284* (New Haven: Yale University Press, 1974), 68ff., and Witherington, *Conflict and Community.*

32. See, e.g., R. P. Martin, *Carmen Christi: Philippians 2:5-11 in Recent Interpretation and in the Setting of Early Christian Worship* (Grand Rapids: Eerdmans, 1983).

33. For a rather convincing attempt to retroject this hymn back into Aramaic, see J. A. Fitzmyer, "The Aramaic Background of Philippians 2:6-11," *Catholic Biblical Quarterly* 50 (1988): 470-83. In view of the hymn's rhythm and rhetorical structure as we now have it in Greek, I am more inclined to think it was originally composed in Greek.

34. Witherington, *Jesus the Sage,* 257-66. I would urge that the primary background for the first half of the hymn is the Wisdom material such as one finds in Proverbs 8:22ff. and elsewhere, while the second half evidently owes something to the servant songs of Isaiah, particularly Isaiah 45, which is quoted, and Isaiah 53. The allusions to Adam and Genesis 1-3 are much more remote, if they exist at all. For a critique of the Adamic argument of J. D. G. Dunn, see my discussion mentioned above and Fowl, *Story of Christ,* 71ff. Dunn's reliance on the *res rapienda* view of *harpagmos* is a weakness, and furthermore Adam did not choose to take on a human nature, as Christ is said to have done in Philippians 2. See O'Brien, *Commentary on Philippians* (Grand Rapids: Eerdmans, 1991), 263-68.

35. See G. H. R. Horsley, *New Documents Illustrating Early Christianity* (Macquarrie: Macquarrie University Press, 1987), 1:83.

36. Silva, *Philippians,* 114ff. is right that the phrases "form of God" and "the being equal to God" are closely related and speak of the same reality.

37. R. W. Hoover, "The Harpagmos Enigma: A Philological Solution," *Harvard Theological Review* 64 (1971): 118.

38. Hawthorne, *Philippians,* 85ff.

39. Witherington, *Paul's Narrative Thought World.*

40. Silva, *Philippians,* 127-28.

41. See L. W. Hurtado, "Jesus as Lordly Example in Philippians 2:5-11," in P. Richardson and J. C. Hurd, eds., *From Jesus to Paul: Studies in Honor of F. W. Beare* (Waterloo, Ont.: Wilfred Laurier University Press, 1984), 125.

42. Ibid.

43. In the Jewish tradition the divine Name was believed to have in and of itself great power, such that the mere pronouncing of it could produce dramatic results. Probably John 18:6 reflects this belief, where

the soldiers fall back when Jesus pronounces the Divine Name. On this text see my forthcoming commentary on John.

44. See N. T. Wright, *The Climax of the Covenant* (Edinburgh: T. & T. Clark, 1991), 120-36.

45. So Silva, *Philippians*, 131.

46. Marshall, *Philippians*, 55.

47. See the discussion in D. B. Martin, *Slavery as Salvation: The Metaphor of Slavery in Pauline Christianity* (New Haven: Yale University Press, 1990), 130-31.

48. John Chrysostom, "Homily 6 on Phil. 2:5-8," in P. Schaff, ed., *The Nicene and Post-Nicene Fathers* (Grand Rapids: Eerdmans, 1976), 206-12.

49. Lightfoot, *Philippians*, 113, makes the interesting point that Paul must have felt this paradox keenly since he as a Roman citizen could not himself have suffered crucifixion and so could not completely follow the model of Christ in this regard.

50. Barclay, "Great Themes," 43.

51. D. F. Watson, "A Rhetorical Analysis of Philippians and Its Implications for the Unity Question," *Novum Testamentum* 30 (1988): 70-71.

52. See Silva, *Philippians*, 134.

53. Watson, "Rhetorical Analysis," 70.

54. See among others J. H. Michael, "Work Out Your Own Salvation," *The Expositor* 9th series 12 (1924): 439-50; Hawthorne, *Philippians*, 97ff.

55. See the discussion in Marshall, *Philippians*, 61.

56. See Exodus 15:16, Isaiah 9:16; in Paul, see 1 Corinthians 2:3, 2 Corinthians 7:15, Ephesians 6:5, and the detailed study in S. Pedersen, "Mit Furcht und Zittern (Phil. 2:12-13)," *Studia Theologia* 32 (1978): 1-31. The explanation that this phrase has a purely human reference ignores the OT background and also the fact that Paul has just mentioned God working in their midst. While 1 Corinthians 2:3 may refer to an interhuman reaction, the other two references from the Pauline corpus suggest that the fear and trembling comes about because of whom the human agents represent and whose authority they act under, namely, God's.

57. As Fowl, *Story of Christ*, 97, notes, this phrase is normally used to discuss the social relationship not between equals but between a superior and some inferiors, whether master and slave as in Ephesians 6, or in this case God and the people of God. O. Glombitza, "Mit Furcht und Zittern: Zum Verständnis von Philip. 2:12," *Novum Testamentum* 3 (1959): 100-106, argues that the phrase does not have to do with the attitude of the community when considering that God is watching them, but suggests consideration for the community. He also toys with the idea that we connect the "not" at the beginning of the clause with the phrase "with fear and trembling," but the Greek order of the

words surely does not favor this, and the context implies some sort of connection with the fact that God is working in the community.

58. See Garland, "Composition and Unity of Philippians," 145ff.

59. See R. M. Oglivie, *The Romans and Their Gods in the Age of Augustus* (New York: Norton and Co., 1969), 47ff. The pouring of wine over the head of a pagan sacrifice was apparently optional and would be seen as an extra sacrificial act.

60. See Silva, *Philippians,* 151.

61. O'Brien, *Philippians,* 310.

62. See Craddock, *Philippians,* 44-45.

63. See Marshall, *Philippians,* 65, on the force of the phrase.

64. Hawthorne, *Philippians,* xxxviiff.

Chapter Seven:
The *Probatio* — 2:1-4:3:
The Second Appeal — 2:19-30

1. D. F. Watson, "A Rhetorical Analysis of Philippians and Its Implications for the Unity Question," *Novum Testamentum* 30 (1988): 71.

2. See R. A. Culpepper, "Co-Workers in Suffering, Philippians 2:19-30," *Review and Expositor* 77 (1980): 349-57; P. T. O'Brien, *Commentary on Philippians* (Grand Rapids: Eerdmans, 1991), 313ff.

3. See R. W. Funk, *Language, Hermeneutic, and the Word of God* (New York: Harper and Row, 1966), 267-68, 71-74. The term "apostolic *parousia*" refers to the coming or presence of the apostle, whether in person or as a presence conveyed through the rhetorical performance of a letter like Philippians, or perhaps through the Holy Spirit (see 1 Cor. 5:4). As an epistolary device, the apostolic *parousia* can refer to the discussion in a letter of the coming or presence of the apostle.

4. T. Y. Mullin, "Visit Talk in New Testament Letters," *Catholic Biblical Quarterly* 35 (1973): 350-58.

5. F. F. Bruce, *Philippians* (New York: Harper & Row, 1983), 73, sees that Paul presents three examples for the Philippians to follow in this section, but strangely argues that Paul did not deliberately set out to do so.

6. So Bruce, *Philippians,* 69.

7. P. Christou, "*Isopsuchos,* Phil. 2:20," *Journal of Biblical Literature* 70 (1951): 293-96.

8. See Culpepper, "Co-workers in Suffering," 353; I. H. Marshall, *Philippians* (London: Epworth, 1991), 69.

9. B. Witherington, *Conflict and Community in Corinth: A Socio-Rhetorical Commentary on 1 and 2 Corinthians* (Grand Rapids: Eerdmans, 1994).

10. As B. Mayer, "Paulus als Vermittler zwischen Epaphroditus und der Gemeinde von Philippi, Bemerkungen zu Phil 2, 25–30," *Biblische Zeitschrift* 31 (1987): 183 suggests, it appears the Philippians had heard of Epaphroditus's illness but were in doubt as to whether or not he had managed to deliver the gift. Paul's delay in writing back to thank them may have been because he was waiting for Epaphroditus to get well enough to travel and carry his letter explaining things back to them so that they would not misread the situation.

11. As J. B. Lightfoot, *St. Paul's Epistle to the Philippians* (London: Macmillan, 1894), 122, notes, Paul uses an ascending scale of terms to refer to Epaphroditus: he shares a common sympathy, a common work, and a common danger as a soldier of Christ. It is interesting, as L. G. Bloomquist, *The Function of Suffering in Philippians* (Sheffield: JSOT Press, 1993), 175, points out, that the same three terms applied here to Epaphroditus recur in Philemon 1–2 (applied to three different people). Bloomquist, however, influenced by D. Patte, once again overreads the undercurrent here when he sees Epaphroditus as another example of what it means to submit to necessity.

12. See the discussion of the term *apostolos* in Witherington, *Conflict and Community*, 203–8.

13. That the congregation sent him also suggests there were other leaders as well, those whom Paul addressed as *episkopoi* and *diakonoi* in Philippians 1:1.

14. It would appear unlikely that Epaphroditus was a slave in view of the various things said about him. Indeed it seems more likely that he was a person of higher status who had the time and freedom to travel, probably at his own expense. It is clear that Paul believes the Philippians think Epaphroditus is extremely valuable.

15. On the prevalence of the name Epaphroditus, as opposed to the less common Epaphras, and the importance of distinguishing these two persons, see G. H. R. Horsley, *New Documents Illustrating Early Christianity*, vol. 4 (Macquarrie: Macquarrie University Press, 1987), 22–23.

16. The term *leitourgos* and its cognate *leitourgia* normally have religious overtones, even when they refer to a public servant, public minister, or public service. The second term can refer to worship, a sacrifice, or an offering, while the first term can refer to a religious figure, but does not necessarily do so. In our text, the term *leitourgos* likely suggests that Epaphroditus has been commissioned to perform a ministry or religious service on behalf of Paul.

17. C. O. Buchanan, "Epaphroditus' Sickness and the Letter to the Philippians," *Evangelical Quarterly* 36 (1964): 157–66.

18. G. Caird, *Paul's Letters from Prison* (Oxford: Oxford University Press, 1976), 129.

19. Buchanan, "Epaphroditus' Sickness," 159, suggests somewhere in northwest Greece.

20. Some have read this passage to require three or four trips between the sending of the gift and Paul's response, including a trip from Rome (or someplace else) to Philippi to inform the Philippians about Epaphroditus' illness, and word brought back that they had heard of this illness. All of this is predicated on the unproven assumption that Epaphroditus first fell ill where Paul was and then word traveled back from there. I would suggest that Philippians 4:22 implies a regular network of communication between where Paul is and Philippi, and this not only favors a Roman location for Paul, but also provides a basis for the conjecture that word about Epaphroditus's illness could have been sent back along the Egnatian Way by some Christian traveling east to or through Philippi.

21. Possibly a courier for the imperial household who was a Christian going to Philippi; see Philippians 4:22.

22. B. S. MacKay, "Further Thoughts on Philippians," *New Testament Studies* 7 (1960–61): 165ff.

23. There is a rather exact parallel, using the epistolary aorist, to the phraseology of Philippians 2:25 in P. Oxy. 2191.

24. See M. Silva, *Philippians* (Grand Rapids: Baker, 1992), 163.

25. O'Brien, *Philippians,* 315.

26. B. Holmberg, *Paul and Power* (Philadelphia: Fortress, 1978), 60.

Chapter Eight:
The *Probatio* — 2:1–4:3:
The Third Appeal — 3:1–4:1

1. I tend to agree with A. E. Harvey, "The Opposition to Paul," in F. L. Cross, ed., *Studia Evangelia* (Berlin: Akademie Verlag, 1968), 4:319-32, that the Judaizers were in essence insisting that all Christians conform to the outward pattern of Jewish religious observance, including the practice of circumcision. The issue was a way of living religiously, but Paul saw the underlying theological problems with such an approach and addressed them. It is a mistake to assume that all of the opposition to Paul was of this sort. In particular in 2 Corinthians Paul seems to be dealing with a different kind of opposition (see B. Witherington, *Conflict and Community in Corinth: A Socio-Rhetorical Commentary on 1 and 2 Corinthians* (Grand Rapids: Eerdmans, 1994). Nevertheless, Judaizers seem to have been the main bane of Paul's existence.

2. L. G. Bloomquist, *The Function of Suffering in Philippians* (Sheffield: JSOT Press, 1993), 178.

3. Ibid., 196.

4. F. Craddock, *Philippians* (Atlanta: John Knox, 1985), 53, rightly points out that just as the function of the Christ hymn in Philippians 2 is parenetic, so too is the autobiographical data in this chapter. It reveals what Paul is willing to count as loss in order to be found in Christ.

5. Notice the *sun* (with) compound words here, as well as other words that stress sharing something in common, as part of Paul's strategy to create unity among the Philippians. He stresses what he and the Philippians share in common, what they all share in common with Christ, and what the Philippians share in common with each other. Note *koinōnia* in v. 10; *summimetai* in v. 17; *summorphon*.

6. D. Stanley, "Imitation in Paul's Letters: Its Significance for His Relationship to Jesus and to His Own Christian Foundations," in P. Richardson and J. C. Hurd, eds., *From Jesus to Paul: Studies in Honor of F. W. Beare* (Waterloo, Ont.: Wilfred Laurier University Press, 1984), 137.

7. See D. F. Watson, "A Rhetorical Analysis of Philippians and Its Implications for the Unity Question," *Novum Testamentum* 30 (1988): 72–75.

8. M. Silva, *Philippians* (Grand Rapids: Baker, 1992), 178. See the more extensive arguments in A. T. Lincoln, *Paradise Now and Not Yet* (Cambridge: Cambridge University Press, 1981), 88–89.

9. Craddock, *Philippians,* 58, emphasis added.

10. G. Caird, *Paul's Letters from Prison* (Oxford: Oxford University Press, 1976), 132.

11. See M. E. Thrall, *Greek Particles in the New Testament: Linguistic and Exegetical Studies* (Leiden: E. J. Brill, 1962), 28; C. F. D. Moule, *An Idiom Book of the New Testament* (Cambridge: Cambridge University Press, 1953), 161–62.

12. B. S. MacKay, "Further Thoughts on Philippians," *New Testament Studies* 7 (1960–61): 161–70.

13. Against the theory of lost Philippian letters see J. B. Lightfoot, *St. Paul's Epistle to the Philippians* (London: Macmillan, 1894), 138–42.

14. G. D. Kilpatrick, "*Blepete,* Philippians 3:2," in M. Black and G. Fohrer, eds., *In Memoriam Paul Kahle* (Berlin: A. Töpelmann, 1968), 145–48.

15. See Caird, *Paul's Letters,* 132–33. His compromise translation "look out for," which would not necessarily convey the idea of the opponents being currently in Philippi, may be possible.

16. The latter literally means "to cut around."

17. One may compare the typical Jewish way of talking about the genitals by using the circumlocutions that we find in 1 Corinthians 12:23, where these parts are called unpresentable; more importantly, Paul uses honor-shame language, as he does here, to describe these

parts. They are "the parts that we think are less honorable." One may also compare Paul's feelings about nakedness in 2 Corinthians 5:3–4, though there nakedness is used as a metaphor for being without the physical body. See B. Witherington, *Jesus, Paul and the End of the World* (Downers Grove, Ill.: InterVarsity Press, 1992), 205ff.

18. H. Koester, "The Purpose of the Polemic of a Pauline Fragment," *New Testament Studies* 8 (1961–62): 317–32. Koester, however, argues that the opponents were also pneumatics (and thus early Gnostics of a sort) on the basis of a very dubious interpretation of 3:3, taking it to mean "we are those who serve as missionaries in the Spirit of God." Strongly against this view is the fact that we have three participles in parallel here: *latreuontes*, "glorifying," and "trusting," which surely favors translating the first participle as "worshiping."

19. The argument by K. Grayston, "The Opponents in Philippians 3," *Expository Times* 97 (1986): 170–72, that they are Gentiles, because Paul uses the term "dogs," fails to recognize the subtle way that Paul will frequently use words in a non-traditional way and apply them to an unexpected audience. In this very passage Paul also calls the church made up of Gentiles and Jews "the circumcision."

20. Pace G. Hawthorne, *Philippians* (Waco, Tex.: Word, 1983), 122ff.

21. Rightly, I. H. Marshall, *Philippians* (London: Epworth, 1991), 100: "The clear implication is that these people were liable to be taken as examples to follow by the Christians at Philippi; therefore they were people who presented themselves as Christians."

22. B. Witherington, *Women in the Earliest Churches* (Cambridge: Cambridge University Press, 1988), 147–49.

23. See the discussion by Lincoln, *Paradise Now*, 87–109.

24. Witherington, *Jesus, Paul and the End of the World*, 100ff.

25. See J. B. Polhill, "Twin Obstacles in the Christian Path," *Review and Expositor* 77 (1980): 362.

26. Marshall, *Philippians*, 85.

27. Craddock, *Philippians*, 59.

28. B. Witherington, *Paul's Narrative Thought World: The Tapestry of Triumph and Tragedy* (Louisville: Westminster/John Knox, 1994).

29. The arguments by Silva, *Philippians*, 174–75, are not wholly satisfactory when he stresses that Paul is talking only about his public credentials here, not his subjective state of mind as a Jew. This position might be possible if it were a third-person reflection on Paul's life and lifestyle, but in fact these are Paul's own reflections on his life and must necessarily indicate how his own pre-Christian conscience led him to evaluate his life as a Pharisee.

30. It is applied generally in one sense or another to food (see Plutarch *Moralia* 352D) and to human excrement (see Josephus *Wars*

5.13.7), but is also used of the scraps left over from a feast and thrown out to the animals. See Lightfoot, *Philippians*, 149, and references there.

31. See Polhill, "Twin Obstacles," 364.

32. Lightfoot, *Philippians*, 149.

33. On Paul as a possible widower or one separated from his wife, see Witherington, *Women in the Earliest Churches*, 30ff.

34. Witherington, *Paul's Narrative Thought World*.

35. Pace Silva, *Philippians*, 186-87.

36. Witherington, *Jesus, Paul and the End of the World*, 186ff.

37. Craddock, *Philippians*, 61.

38. Witherington, *Conflict and Community*.

39. Marshall, *Philippians*, 95.

40. Ibid., 98. The danger he is referring to is that of claiming a premature perfection different from Paul's vision of perfection, which is full conformity to the image of Christ by gaining a resurrection body like his.

41. Craddock, *Philippians*, 68.

42. For further discussion on the fact that Paul is opposing Judaizers throughout this passage, see Lincoln, *Paradise Now*, 95ff.

43. Ibid., 98-99.

44. Ibid., 100.

45. S. E. Fowl, *The Story of Christ in the Ethics of Paul* (Sheffield: JSOT Press, 1990), 49ff.

46. O'Brien, *Philippians*, 461.

47. Rightly Fowl, *Story of Christ*, 86.

48. This is found in Hunt-Edgar, *Select Papyri* II, 76, no. 211.

49. A. D. Nock, "Soter and Euegertes," in Z. Stewart, ed., *Essays on Religion and the Ancient World* (Cambridge: Harvard University Press, 1972), 727.

50. Ibid., 720-35.

51. Marshall, *Philippians*, 104.

52. See P. Collart, "Inscriptions de Philippes," *Bulletin du Correspondance hellénique* 57 (1933): 340-41.

53. See the excursus on imperial eschatology in Witherington, *Conflict and Community*, 295-98.

54. See G. H. R. Horsley, *New Documents Illustrating Early Christianity* (Macquarrie: Macquarrie University Press, 1987), 2:49.

55. Witherington, *Conflict and Community*.

56. Witherington, *Jesus, Paul and the End of the World*, 183ff.

57. Craddock, *Philippians*, 69.

58. C. R. Holladay, "Paul's Opponents in Philippians 3," *Restoration Quarterly* 12 (1969): 77-90.

Chapter Nine:
The *Probatio* — 2:1–4:3:
The Fourth Appeal — 4:2–3

1. B. Mengel, *Studien zum Philipperbrief* (Tübingen: Mohr, 1982), 280, rightly connects the phrase *to auto phronein en kuriō* here with 2:1–5 and also 1:27–30. Verses 2:1–5 are the background of our discussion, and so this passage is a further development of the appeal to be of one mind, part of the essential *propositio* found in 1:27–30.

2. But see D. Garland, "The Composition and Unity of Philippians," *Novum Testamentum* 27 (1985): 173.

3. D. F. Watson, "A Rhetorical Analysis of Philippians and Its Implications for the Unity Question," *Novum Testamentum* 30 (1988): 76–77.

4. On the *parakalō* periods in Paul's letters, see C. J. Bjerkelund, *Parakalo: Form, Funktion und Sinn der parakalo-Sätze in den paulinischen Briefen* (Oslo: Universitetsforlaget, 1967).

5. B. Witherington, *Women in the Earliest Churches* (Cambridge: Cambridge University Press, 1988), 111–13.

6. D. Ezell, "The Sufficiency of Christ: Philippians 4," *Review and Expositor* 77 (1980): 375.

7. G. Hawthorne, *Philippians* (Waco, Tex.: Word, 1983), 180.

8. F. X. Malinowski, "The Brave Women of Philippi," *Biblical Theology Bulletin* 15 (1985): 60–63. He is right, however, that the term suggests that whenever Euodia and Syntyche did this struggling, it is implied that there was considerable opposition to Paul and the gospel at that time. 2 Corinthians 8:2 strikes several familiar notes: (1) the churches (note the plural, which probably suggests at least those in Thessalonica as well) had a severe ordeal of affliction; (2) they gave generously to the Collection despite their poverty; and (3) they had abundant joy, even in spite of their circumstances. Since all three of these notes are also found in Philippians, it seems likely that Paul has the church or churches there primarily in view in 2 Corinthians 8. This passage was likely written in the period 55–58, and so perhaps two to four years prior to Philippians.

9. See F. F. Bruce, *Philippians* (New York: Harper & Row, 1983), 115.

10. See G. H. R. Horsley, *New Documents Illustrating Early Christianity* (Macquarrie: Macquarrie University Press, 1987), 1:54.

11. See J. B. Lightfoot, *St. Paul's Epistle to the Philippians* (London: Macmillan, 1894), 158–59.

12. W. W. Tarn and G. W. Griffith, *Hellenistic Civilisation*, 3d ed. (London: E. Arnold, 1952), 98.

13. See D. Schaps, "The Woman Least Mentioned: Etiquette and Women's Names," *Classical Quarterly* 27 (1977): 323–30.

14. *New Documents*, 4:178–79.

15. See J. Wiseman, "A Distinguished Macedonian Family of the Roman Imperial Period," *American Journal Archaeology* 88 (1984): 567–82, for one example.

16. A. J. Marshall, "Roman Women and the Provinces," *Ancient Society* 6 (1975): 108–27.

17. On officials' wives in the provinces; see Tacitus *Agr.* 6.3, 45.4, in this case in Asia.

18. Marshall, "Roman Women," 117.

19. A. H. Smith, "Notes on a Tour of Asia Minor," *Journal of Hellenic Studies* 8 (1887): 256, n. 41.

20. See Marshall, "Roman Women," 125.

21. R. MacMullen, "Women in Public in the Roman Empire," *Historia* 29, no. 2 (1980): 208–18.

22. Marshall, *Philippians,* 110: "It may be significant that, where there was apparently no synagogue, and where the more liberal attitudes of the Macedonians may have prevailed, the church developed some female leadership. It may well be that the factor which prevented more widespread development was Jewish influence within other first-century churches."

23. Schaps, "Woman Least Mentioned," 328ff.

24. On women of wealth in the provinces, see R. Van Bremen, "Women and Wealth," in *Images of Women in Antiquity,* ed. A. Cameron and A. Kuhrt (Detroit: Wayne State University Press, 1983), 223–42.

25. B. Witherington, *Conflict and Community in Corinth: A Socio-Rhetorical Commentary on 1 and 2 Corinthians* (Grand Rapids: Eerdmans, 1994).

26. Marshall, *Philippians,* 108.

27. M. Silva, *Philippians* (Grand Rapids: Baker, 1992), 221.

28. As Lightfoot, *Philippians,* 159, notes, Revelation 3:5 makes quite clear that this phrase does not imply some sort of absolute predestination of individuals to be saved, since one's name can be blotted out of this book of life.

29. F. Craddock, *Philippians* (Atlanta: John Knox, 1985), 70.

Chapter Ten:
The *Peroratio* — 4:4–20
Division I — 4:4–9

1. See D. Ezell, "The Sufficiency of Christ: Philippians 4," *Review and Expositor* 77 (1980): 376. It means something like justice tempered with mercy in a forensic context.

2. D. F. Watson, "A Rhetorical Analysis of Philippians and Its Implications for the Unity Question," *Novum Testamentum* 30 (1988): 77.

3. The verb is a present imperative indicating ongoing and continuous activity. See P. T. O'Brien, *Commentary on Philippians* (Grand Rapids: Eerdmans, 1991), 507, n. 42.

4. Ezell, "Sufficiency of Christ," 376.

5. O'Brien, *Philippians*, 485.

6. I. H. Marshall, *Philippians* (London: Epworth, 1991), 111.

7. B. Witherington, *Jesus, Paul and the End of the World* (Downers Grove, Ill.: InterVarsity Press, 1992), 33. The argument of many that we have a sequence of purely isolated individual exhortations in 4:4ff. is not fully convincing, especially in view of the *kai* that connects vv. 6 and 7, and another that connects vv. 8 and 9, but see O'Brien, *Philippians*, 483ff., for a discussion of the usual atomistic approach.

8. On echoes of the Psalms in Paul's writings, see the forthcoming article on this subject by R. B. Hays, and for the general idea consult his book, *Echoes of Scripture in the Letters of Paul* (New Haven: Yale University Press, 1989).

9. See Marshall, *Philippians*, 112, for the suggestion that *maranatha* lies in the background here. I doubt this because in Philippians we have the verb "to be," not the verb "to come" as in the early Aramaic wish prayer found in 1 Corinthians 16:22.

10. J. S. Stewart, "Old Texts in Modern Translations, Philippians 4:6, 7 (Moffatt)," *Expository Times* 49 (1937–38): 269–71.

11. Rightly, M. Silva, *Philippians* (Grand Rapids: Baker, 1992), 225.

12. O'Brien, *Philippians*, 498.

13. Ibid.

14. Silva, *Philippians*, 230.

15. It is extremely instructive to compare what Paul says here to what his near contemporary Plutarch says about virtue in various contexts. Like Paul, Plutarch disagrees with the Stoics about the relationship between virtue and passion, and like Paul (in Philippians), Plutarch in his famous *Parallel Lives* seeks to hold up moral examples to emulate or shun. There are numerous ways in which Paul and Plutarch disagree with each other, however. Plutarch, unlike the Stoics, does not believe in the necessity of radical conversion for a person to become good or wise. His is a theory of moral progress and gradualism. See the helpful collection in H. D. Betz, *Plutarch's Ethical Writings and Early Christian Literature* (Leiden: Brill, 1978), especially the essays by W. C. Grese on "De profectibus in Virtute," 11–31; by K. O'Brien-Wicker on "Mulierum Virtutes," 106–34, and most importantly J. P. Hershbell, "De Virtute Morali," 135–69.

16. As J. B. Lightfoot, *St. Paul's Epistle to the Philippians* (London: Macmillan, 1894), 162, suggests when he paraphrases, " 'Whatever value may reside in your old heathen conception of virtue'...as if the Apostle were anxious not to omit any possible ground of appeal."

17. So L. Michael White, "Morality between Worlds: A Paradigm of Friendship in Philippians," in D. L. Balch et al., eds., *Greeks, Romans, and Christians* (Minneapolis: Fortress, 1990), 203.

18. See G. H. R. Horsley, *New Documents Illustrating Early Christianity* (Macquarrie: Macquarrie University Press, 1987), 4:171, for the use of this term in pagan epitaphs; it is *not* found in pagan virtue lists. See O'Brien, *Philippians,* 505.

19. O'Brien, *Philippians,* 501.

20. For example, J. N. Sevenster, *Paul and Seneca* (Leiden: Brill, 1961), 152–56; R. P. Martin, *Carmen Christi: Philippians 2:5–11 in Recent Interpretation and in the Setting of Early Christian Worship* (Grand Rapids: Eerdmans, 1983), 157–58, though Martin is not fully convinced it would seem (see p. 32).

21. O'Brien, *Philippians,* 508.

22. See the example from the papyri in *New Documents,* 1:58. It can also have the sense of "furthermore," and even "in future"; see *New Documents,* 4:67.

23. See O'Brien, *Philippians,* 499. B. Mengel, *Studien zum Philipperbrief* (Tübingen: Mohr, 1982), 281–82, sees *to loipon* as a means of connecting the general Greco-Roman parenesis in v. 8 with the more specific reference to the church's ethical tradition in 4:4–7.

24. Such as anaphora, asyndeton, polysyndeton, and homioteleuton. See the detailed discussion and explanation of these devices in G. Hawthorne, *Philippians* (Waco, Tex.: Word, 1983), 185–90.

25. The word *semna* often appears on pagan funerary inscriptions; see *New Documents,* 3:40–41.

26. A conditional statement the form of which assumes that the condition is true — *ei* (if) plus the present tense of the verb.

27. See Silva, *Philippians,* 229: "We must understand Paul's list as representing distinctly Christian virtues (though we need not deny that many non-Christian citizens exemplify such virtues in their lives)."

28. B. Witherington, *The Christology of Jesus* (Minneapolis: Fortress, 1990), 12ff.

29. J. Paul Sampley, *Pauline Partnership in Christ: Christian Community and Commitment in Light of Roman Law* (Philadelphia: Fortress, 1980).

30. White, "Morality between Worlds," 201–15.

31. See Horsley's critique in *New Documents,* 1:19; White, in "Morality between Worlds," 210–12; and Peterman, "Giving and Receiving in Paul's Epistles: Greco-Roman Social Conventions in Philippians and Other Pauline Writings," Ph.D. diss., King's College, University of London, 1992, forthcoming in the Society for New Testament Studies monograph series from Cambridge University Press, esp. 228–33.

32. Horsley, *New Documents,* 1:19.

33. Peterman, "Giving and Receiving," 232.

34. Ibid., 231.

35. White, "Morality between the Worlds," 210–13.

36. See the discussion in P. Garnsey and R. Saller, *The Roman Empire: Economy, Society, and Culture* (Berkeley: University of California Press, 1987), 107–59.

37. As White, "Morality between Worlds," 214 and n. 58, acknowledges.

38. W. P. De Boer, *The Imitation of Paul: An Exegetical Study* (Kampen: Kok, 1962), 184ff.

39. Ibid., 186–87.

40. F. Craddock, *Philippians* (Atlanta: John Knox, 1985), 74.

Chapter Eleven:
The *Peroratio* — 4:4–20
Division II — 4:10–20

1. The financial flavor of this whole passage has long been recognized. See H. A. A. Kennedy, "The Financial Colouring of Philippians 4:15–18," *Expository Times* 12 (1900): 43–44, as an early example.

2. For instance, compare how Paul handles the matter of his request to Philemon in the letter of the same name.

3. G. J. Bahr, "The Subscription in the Pauline Letters," *Journal of Biblical Literature* 87 (1968): 38.

4. Ibid., 31–32. For a near contemporary example of a record in letter form, see Cicero, *ad Famil.* 13.28A (written 46 B.C.E.).

5. L. G. Bloomquist, *The Function of Suffering in Philippians* (Sheffield: JSOT Press, 1993), 190.

6. B. Witherington, *Conflict and Community in Corinth: A Socio-Rhetorical Commentary on 1 and 2 Corinthians* (Grand Rapids: Eerdmans, 1994).

7. See ibid., on 1 Corinthians 9.

8. On Christians and hospitality, see J. B. Mathews, *Hospitality and the New Testament* (Ann Arbor: University Microfilms, 1965), 165ff. Mathews presents some evidence that hospitality was generally on the decline during the early Empire, which may have made the Christian provision of this needed commodity all the more important for Paul and other traveling missionaries.

9. Witherington, *Conflict and Community.*

10. On this whole subject, consult R. F. Hock, *The Social Context of Paul's Ministry* (Philadelphia: Fortress, 1980). Hock's attempt to make Paul's working an all-encompassing explanation of his missionary *modus operandi* does not convince. Paul accepted various sorts of support, as we have discussed above, and he also traveled a great deal even

without support. There is no evidence, for example, that Paul worked while in Philippi or in Galatia.

11. I am indebted to the helpful discussion by G. W. Peterman, "Giving and Receiving in Paul's Epistles: Greco-Roman Social Conventions in Philippians and other Pauline Writings," Ph.D. diss., King's College, University of London, 1992, forthcoming in the Society for New Testament Studies monograph series from Cambridge University Press, 180ff.

12. On the translation of this verse, see N. Baumert, "1st Philipper 4,10 richtig übersetzt?" *Biblische Zeitschrift* 13 (1969): 256–63.

13. On this translation, see L. Morris, "*Kai hapax kai dis,*" *Novum Testamentum* 1 (1956): 208.

14. I. H. Marshall, *Philippians* (London: Epworth, 1991), 118.

15. P. T. O'Brien, *Commentary on Philippians* (Grand Rapids: Eerdmans, 1991), 514.

16. F. Craddock, *Philippians* (Atlanta: John Knox, 1985), 75–76.

17. J. Weiss, *Beiträge zur Paulinischen Rhetorik* (Göttingen: Vandenhoeck & Ruprecht, 1897), 29. For a very detailed analysis of the carefully composed structure of this passage, see W. Schenk, *Die Philipperbriefe des Paulus* (Stuttgart: Kohlhammer, 1984), 29ff.

18. See the discussion in O'Brien, *Philippians,* 516ff.

19. Even though Epaphroditus is the Philippians' agent, Paul has the authority and power to send him back. This too little noticed fact shows rather clearly the way the social networks operated in Paul's churches. Paul has ultimate authority over them all, even though several years and numerous miles removed. His partnership with the Philippians is not one of complete equality. He is the senior partner and has the power to override, correct, or reverse decisions made at the local level.

20. M. Silva, *Philippians* (Grand Rapids: Baker, 1992), 231.

21. For a critique of the "thankless thanks" view of this passage, see B. Mengel, *Studien zum Philipperbrief* (Tübingen: Mohr, 1982), 282–85.

22. See O. Glombitza, "Der Dank des Apostels: Zum Verständnis von Philipper 4:10–20," *Novum Testamentum* 7 (1964–65): 135–41, for the suggestion that Paul is implying here that he, like all Christians, is only ultimately dependent on grace alone.

23. P. Marshall, *Enmity in Corinth: Social Conventions in Paul's Relations with the Corinthians* (Tübingen: Mohr, 1987), 159.

24. This may in part reflect the fact that Paul, as a well-educated Roman citizen, had been a person of high status, for whom it was a matter of swallowing one's pride and counting as loss one's former assets in order to accept gifts from churches, some of which were impoverished. See E. A. Judge, "The Social Identity of the First Christians," *Journal of Religious History* 1 (1960): 201–17, who says that the "status opportu-

nities Paul declined remain the measure of his potential professional standing, and of the expectation of his supporters for him. The extent of his renunciation helps to explain Paul's intense consciousness of debasement. He was stepping firmly down in the world" (214).

25. O'Brien, *Philippians*, 510.

26. F. F. Bruce, *Philippians* (New York: Harper & Row, 1983), 123, emphasis added.

27. See Marshall, *Enmity*, 34ff. I suspect these conventions came into play in Corinth when he refused patronage while there; see Witherington, *Conflict and Community*.

28. See R. P. Saller, *Personal Patronage under the Early Empire* (Cambridge: Cambridge University Press, 1982).

29. The phrase *hapax kai dis*, literally "once and twice," means "more than once." See Morris, "*Kai hapax kai dis*," 205-8. If, as O'Brien, *Philippians*, 563, and Morris aver, the first *kai* is a true connective, then there is also reference to aid received elsewhere. Perhaps Corinth is in view (see 2 Cor. 11:8-9).

30. Silva, *Philippians*, 234.

31. O'Brien, *Philippians*, 521.

32. On the use of *koinōnia* here, see M. Jack Suggs, "*Koinōnia* in the New Testament," *Mid-Stream* 23 (1984): 352-54. Suggs is right to point to the close connections between 1:5 and 4:15, and 1:7 and 4:12, 14, which is yet another argument that 4:10-20 should be seen as part of the same letter as Philippians 1, bringing its arguments and issues to a close.

33. E. Lohmeyer, *Der Brief an die Philipper, an die Kolosser und an Philemon* (Göttingen: Vandenhoeck & Ruprecht, 1956), 182ff., attempts to read the whole letter, including this verse, in a martyrological light, but this is overpressing the text here.

34. See W. M. Ramsay, "Notes II. On the Greek Form of the Name Philippians," *Journal of Theological Studies* 1 (1900): 116.

35. O'Brien, *Philippians*, 531.

36. Would some in Rome have concluded that Paul took pay for proclaiming the Word, and so he too proclaimed it out of selfish ambition, as Paul claims about others in 1:15-18?

37. See M. J. Suggs, "Concerning the Date of Paul's Macedonian Ministry," *Novum Testamentum* 4 (1960): 60-68.

38. Too much has been made about Paul's crossing over in Europe, as if crossing the Hellespont would have been seen by Paul as a watershed event, breaking new ministerial ground. Here Suggs, "Concerning the Date," 63, is right to complain. In Paul's day Asia and Macedonia were simply areas in two different Roman provinces, closely united by a common language and Roman control. It is anachronistic to speak

of Paul going to a new continent when he went to Philippi, since he would not have seen such significance in the act.

39. But see O. Glombitza, "Der Dank des Apostels: Zum Verständnis von Philipper iv. 10–20," *Novum Testamentum* 7 (1964–65): 135–41.

40. Lohmeyer, *Der Brief an die Philipper,* 184–85.

41. O'Brien, *Philippians,* 532.

42. Peterman, "Giving and Receiving," 163ff.; see also Marshall, *Enmity,* 157–64.

43. But see Lohmeyer, *Der Brief an die Philipper,* 185.

44. See especially J. Paul Sampley, *Pauline Partnership in Christ: Christian Community and Commitment in Light of Roman Law* (Philadelphia: Fortress, 1980), 55.

45. Peterman, "Giving and Receiving," 166–67.

46. Lohmeyer, *Der Brief an die Philipper,* 186, may be right that the word *karpon,* literally "fruit," may have its eschatological sense here, as elsewhere in Paul.

47. Witherington, *Conflict and Community.*

48. This point favors the view that the phrase "giving and receiving" is being used in a broader more metaphorical sense and not simply of credits and debits in a legal relationship.

49. Paul does not say, for he could not do so, that God will fulfill their (or our) every request, for sometimes believers, even prophets, ask for things not in accord with God's will (e.g., 1 Kings 19:4–10).

50. Marshall, *Philippians,* 122.

51. This point also counts against the negative reading of this passage.

52. See, e.g., the *Res gestae,* column 6, line 25, in R. K. Sherk, *The Roman Empire* (Cambridge: Cambridge University Press, 1988), 50.

53. Consult Witherington, *Conflict and Community,* 295–98, on the use of the term "Father" in Roman imperial propaganda and eschatology.

Chapter 12:
Epistolary Closing/Subscription — 4:21–23

1. G. J. Bahr, "The Subscription in the Pauline Letters," *Journal of Biblical Literature* 87 (1968): 40–41.

2. On the form of ancient letters, see S. K. Stowers, *Letter Writing in Greco-Roman Antiquity* (Philadelphia: Westminster, 1986); F. X. J. Exler, *The Form of the Ancient Greek Letter of the Epistolary Papyri (3rd c. B.C.– 3rd c. A.D.* (Chicago: Ares Publisher, 1976).

3. G. Hawthorne, *Philippians* (Waco, Tex.: Word, 1983), 212ff.

4. See the judicious discussion of older views in J. B. Lightfoot, *St. Paul's Epistle to the Philippians* (London: Macmillan, 1894), 171–78.

5. P. C. Weaver, *Familia Caesaris* (Cambridge: Cambridge University Press, 1972), 295; note the detailed look at the terminology itself on 299–300.

6. Ibid., 296.

7. Ibid., 301-2.

8. C. Hemer, *The Book of Acts in the Setting of Hellenistic History* (Winona Lake, Ind.: Eisenbrauns, 1990), 273-74, conjectures plausibly that the reference in Philippians 4:22 is to Christian couriers within the imperial service who went back and forth between Rome and the colony cities, such as Philippi. He is right that if one is to determine the locale from which Paul wrote this letter, it is most crucial to take into account "routes and opportunities, rather than mere distance" as "the crucial factors, and they point to Rome. Traveling elsewhere was more likely to depend on long delays in chartering a passage."

9. Ibid., 247-53.

10. R. P. Martin, *Carmen Christi: Philippians 2:5-11 in Recent Interpretation and in the Setting of Early Christian Worship* (Grand Rapids: Eerdmans, 1983), 170.

11. Lightfoot, *Philippians*, 172-73.

12. If it could be shown that the Praetorium is meant in Philippians 1:13 then this reference could perhaps be coordinated with what is said here in 4:22, in which case Paul in 1:13 would be alluding to the fact that he had converted some of the civil servants in the household of Caesar. This seems less probable than the conclusion drawn in the text.

13. See G. H. R. Horsley, *New Documents Illustrating Early Christianity* (Macquarrie: Macquarrie University Press, 1987), 2:28.

Index of Biblical Passages

Index of Extra-Biblical References

Index of Modern Authors

Ben Witherington is Professor of Biblical and Wesleyan Studies at Ashland Theological Seminary, Ashland, Ohio, and an ordained United Methodist minister in the Western North Carolina Conference of the United Methodist Church. Among his many books are *Paul's Narrative Thought Word* and *Jesus the Sage: The Pilgrimage of Wisdom.*